The Husky Handbook

The Ultimate Guide for All New Husky Puppy Owners

HARRY EVANS © 2020

My Happy Husky

THE GO TO PLACE FOR ALL
HUSKY OWNERS

www.myhappyhusky.com

Table of Contents

About the Book

Bringing home a new husky puppy is an exciting, life-changing moment. You're about to have a new member in your family so congratulations are definitely due!

I would like to now thank you for choosing to purchase this handbook, which will guide you through everything you need to know for your new husky puppy!

There are many generic puppy training handbooks out there and while they are great resources for some breeds, the Siberian husky is a truly unique breed with characteristics, behavior, and tendencies that are certainly *not* generic. Therefore, a book made solely for the Siberian husky is much needed for anyone welcoming in a new husky puppy to their home.

I intend on making this book to the point and very informative. But where I feel necessary, add in some of my own views and thoughts. After all, it can be easy to get sucked into some kind of automated learning and training routine that you almost force it on to your pup. Why train your puppy like a robot when you can achieve better results by training him with love, appreciation, patience and most importantly, a big smile on your face. Throughout the book I will try to take moments like this where I stop with continuous advice and training to reconnect some emotion. I feel like this is really important because through desperation of having an obedient puppy (which we all want), it's easy to forget to enjoy the complete journey. The complete journey of all the mistakes, mishaps, chewed up socks and the odd explosion of diarrhea. Remember your new puppy, is now your new best friend, he will love you more than you can imagine, so have patience with him and despite being firm with training, continuously ensure you're giving him the warmth and love that he deserves.

The Husky Puppy Handbook: The Ultimate Guide for All New Husky Puppy Owners Is the only book you will need to successfully bring in and raise a new husky puppy.

Welcome to our pack.

As I will be writing this book based on my experience living with Cyborg, a male husky mix living in the Philippines, I will be referring to your pup as **him/he.**

For my short and sweet introduction, I'm Harry, and I am 26-years-old. I started life sleeping on the belly of Gena, a female German shepherd. Up until right now, I have had many dogs continuously present through all my years, and I couldn't have imagined a life without them. From Gena, my German Shepherd, to Rocky and Blake my two Black Labradors, and now Cyborg a Husky Mix.

After years of being obsessed with how all dogs learn, behave and respond to different training styles, I found myself helping a fair amount of people with their own furry friends. After spending a lot of my recent years around Siberian huskies, I decided to create a website called My Happy Husky, as a resource for any husky owner needing to learn more about their beautiful snow dog. After a short while I realized that most questions come from puppy owners, and raising a puppy to be a happy, well-behaved mature dog, is something many people need help with. That's what gave me the idea to write the following handbook. I look forward to your journey and I hope you are able to take away some of the valuable information provided throughout. Thank you.

What to expect from this book

Many of you will be at different stages, so it's challenging to start this book in the correct place for everyone. While this handbook will provide valuable information for all husky puppy owners at practically any stage, **it will mostly benefit those of you who are just about to start the journey.**

This handbook aims to be a complete resource and guide, giving you all the knowledge you need to bring in and raise a happy, obedient husky puppy.

Everything that you need will be here for you, but your success in raising your puppy will depend on your consistency, dedication, focus, and patience that you give to your new best friend.

This handbook won't be of value to you, unless you put the tips, advice and proven techniques into practice, and see it through to the end. All the training techniques in this book are based on proven methods of training Siberian huskies.

To begin with, I'll be covering important information about adoption, followed by a section on breeders. If you already have your husky puppy and you didn't adopt him from a shelter, the next section isn't very relevant to you, but of course, you can still read through if you would like to!

The section after that is all about your breeder and important information to get from them *before* purchasing your pup. If you've already got your puppy home and you have finished your negotiations with your breeder, you may still find some useful information in this section; and upon reading, you may discover some vital things you need to clarify. Hopefully, you have some contact information to reach your breeder.

What to Expect From a New Husky Puppy

Siberian huskies are different from most other breeds, and that's why they deserve a handbook of their own. Generic "dog" advice will not be sufficient for your new little friend.

Huskies are a wonderful breed with a beautiful character. Despite their wolfish looks, Siberians are very friendly and approachable. They get along well with other dogs and strangers. On top of this, they love our company and will make a great addition to your family. So you've got a lot to look forward to.

But, it's important for you to know that with all of those positives, come a few challenges. Huskies are considered one of the hardest breeds to own, and while on some levels I disagree, they didn't exactly get that common opinion from nowhere... It's also why huskies continue to be abandoned across the country at a growing rate. Many would-be husky owners don't quite know what they're getting themselves into.

So what should you expect from your new husky puppy?

Well, in the beginning, like most puppies, you can expect him to sleep, A LOT. But as he grows, he'll become extremely curious, especially with his mouth. Huskies, in general, are heavy chewers and this starts from puppyhood. Nipping, biting and chewing is all on their resume, so be prepared for that.

Huskies are also known for being stubborn and independent, which is certainly true. This behavior can be quite frustrating for owners, more so than you can imagine, but it can be limited if you start training and forming good habits from the first day home. But remember, your husky will have a bold character and it's just a part of the breed. You can view his stubbornness as an issue, or appreciate it for the times that it makes you laugh.

Another well-known trait of Siberian huskies is their incredible energy and desire for intense physical exercise. I like referring to huskies as the ultra-marathon runners of the dog world, capable of running more than 100 miles in a day (and *actually* enjoy it). But, you don't have to worry *too* much right now. As your husky is just a little puppy, he doesn't need that kind of exercise as his body is undergoing important growth and development. Again, I will be going through exactly how to exercise your puppy during his growing stage, so you don't have to take up running *just* yet.

You should expect a journey with your husky puppy, and whether or not it's a good journey will mostly depend upon you. Your patience, time and understanding will be pushed to the limit by your pup. It will seem like he's trying to make the journey as tough as possible, but he's not, it's all part of him growing up and learning along the way. Training will not be easy and he'll try to defy you just like a young teenager would. Remain calm and focus on only enjoying the wonderful experience of raising your new husky puppy; after all, he'll only be a puppy once.

This book will give you all the knowledge you need. It's up to you to put it in to practice.

Huskies From Around the World

So, I decided to have a little bit of fun with this and more importantly, **show my appreciation for the readers of My Happy Husky.**

Throughout the book and at the end you'll meet just some of the awesome huskies from different countries, who all enjoy My Happy Husky articles and content.

So, too all of you, who have supported us from the beginning, and for all future supporters, **thank you.**

Kindest regards, Harry – My Happy Husky

Huskies From Around the World

This is Zuko enjoying his car rides!
He's 5 months old from the United States.

Points about Adoption

Adoption is awesome and I encourage you to adopt if you're willing to. Every dog deserves a warm home and a loving family. Every dog rescued, is one more life saved.

It just so happens that there are A LOT of huskies up for adoption, at pretty much all times.

When it comes to huskies, the sad reality is that they're particularly hard to raise and manage which is why a lot of them end up in animal shelters.

What to know about adopting

It's really important you find out as much information as you can about any particular husky before you adopt him. If the husky you're looking at in the shelter has had a rough past involving animal abuse then you need to be ready for different challenges. While it's important to state that this isn't always the case, there can be a very wide range of behavioral issues that come from huskies who were originally subjected to animal abuse in their past.

This is by no means a reason not to adopt, but it can definitely affect your husky's character, temperament, and trainability later on in life. It's important to be aware of that before taking him home.

Vaccines

Animal shelters typically give vaccines to all dogs and puppies when they arrive to the shelter, but you can't assume this. You'll need to clarify with the shelter exactly what kind of vaccines they have given to the puppy, if any. You'll want to double check this yourself with a vet visit right after you rescue the pup.

First vet visit

If you decide to rescue a puppy from a shelter, you should visit your local veterinarian as soon as possible for a full examination of the puppy's health. The vet will be able to take tests and find out which vaccines have or have not been given, and all health issues, if there are any.

Delayed Behavior Response

I just made that term up, but I like it! One very important thing to remember is that it can take around 7-9 weeks for any rescued puppy/dog to start showing their true behavioral tendencies. This means that it's very hard to fully know what "kind" of puppy you're looking at just from visiting them in the shelter. For any dog, life inside an animal shelter is DRASTICALLY different from life inside a home with a loving family. So how your puppy will adjust is unknown; you would expect it be positive, but that's not *always* the case.

Finding a good animal shelter

It's best to get some recommendations from the local dog owner community to find good animal shelters. You can also check at your local veterinarian practice. Before resulting to Google, which happens to be the last option, I really encourage you to speak to as many people as you can. By speaking to someone who has a dog from any particular shelter, they're able to give valuable information you can't find by just googling "local animal shelters". But, if all of that fails, Google is your next option.

If you don't already have your husky puppy and are currently looking to get one I encourage you to check local animal shelters before settling with a breeder to buy one. You may find the husky of your dreams, and you would literally be saving their life.

But of course, your decision is your decision, and whether you want to rescue a husky, or get one from a breeder is up to you and no one else.

Huskies From Around the World

This is Sheva. She's a little cutie with beautiful markings!
She's from Sweden and she is 5 months old.

MEET *Sheva*

5 MONTHS, FROM SWEDEN !

Important Information about Your Breeder

While you're overdosing on cuteness from a litter of gorgeous husky puppies, it's easy to forget all the necessary things to find out; I've been in the same situations a few times myself. What I have learned is that the breeder is the most important part of this whole process and they have valuable information that you need to know. Some breeders will offer up absolutely everything without you asking, and some will either intentionally or unintentionally forget a few things; hopefully it's the latter.

There's a lot that goes into breeding puppies and being a breeder is a wonderful profession that deserves a lot of respect. It comes with many challenges, learning curves and it's a long journey to fully understand what goes into the entire process. Reputable breeders have likely been in the game for a long time and have built up their trust with local veterinarians and will be known by most of the local dog owner community.

Unfortunately, as it can be a fairly lucrative business, it constantly attracts many illegitimate breeders, trying to make a quick buck. The result of this means you have people breeding dogs together without knowing or caring for the health of the parents, or future puppies. When breeding puppies, the health and safety of the dogs involved and the offspring is the most important aspect of the whole process and requires extensive knowledge. This is completely disregarded when you have people breeding dogs that are just in it for the money.

Finding a breeder

When it comes to finding a breeder, I see it as having two options, you can either find a breeder yourself through word of mouth, speaking with other people, visiting your local veterinarian practice for referrals, or, you can look online.

You have to be particularly careful when looking for a breeder online. I'm not suggesting that all online breeders are shady, and the truth is that they are not. BUT the internet is a place where you can hide behind a screen, and for illegitimate breeders, this is a favorite way to conduct their business. A safe way to use the internet to get a new puppy is when you only use it, to find a breeder that you then go to visit in person. In this day and age we are so used to impulsive decision making that we make purchases online without thinking twice. If you're buying some shampoo, it's no problem, but when you're buying puppy, you're buying a life. To my disbelief I've seen websites with an actual "buy" button for a puppy, which I find so sad.

The other way to find a breeder is through word of mouth and being referred to one by either your local veterinarian practice, or a local dog owner. I much prefer this way and nothing beats being able to speak to someone who actually got their own dog from that breeder. You can find out a lot about a breeder this way, before you even go to visit them. And when you're making such an important decision like getting a new puppy, you want all the information you can get.

Before using google which I'm sure many of you already have, I kindly encourage you to ask around your community, friends, family and especially your local vets.

Once you've found a breeder, you're going to need to know what to ask them, so below is the complete set of questions you need to have ready.

What to ask your breeder?

There are many important questions to ask your breeder and it's best not to skip any of them. The more information you know, the better position you will be in to make a very important life-changing decision. It may be a good reality check to remember that whichever puppy you choose, will be a part of your life, and your family's life, forever.

So here's your checklist of questions that you must ask your breeder.

1. How old are the puppies

Age affects a lot of things and will change how you go about looking after your puppy. You need to know exactly how old the litter is.

Too Young: There are laws that breeders need to follow, and if they are not, it's a warning sign that you need to be aware of. In the US it depends on what state you are in, but most follow the same rule of 8 weeks old. This is the age that puppies are deemed healthy and strong enough to leave their mother. You should check the laws in the state that you are buying your puppy in and be very wary if you come across a breeder who is trying to sell under this age. If you find out this is happening to you, you should ask further questions and perhaps even consider a different breeder.

Too Old: If you're viewing a puppy that's already 12 or 14 weeks old, it can also be a warning sign, especially if all other puppies in that litter have been sold. This may indicate some health issues or behavior issues with this particular puppy, so you'll need to ask your breeder if there are any concerns for this particular puppy.

2. Have the puppies and parents had their full health check-ups? Ask to see the documents

Both parents of the litter need to have had a full, professional health check-up before they were allowed to breed. Your breeder should be able to show you the health documents to prove this. Then, once all the puppies are born, they also need a full health check-up and once again, you should be able to see documentation supporting this.

Try to ask your breeder for more information regarding the parents and find out as much about them as you can. Any behavioral issues that the parents had may be passed down to their offspring. If either the mother or father has aggressive tendencies, it makes it very possible for the puppies to develop some level of aggression as they grow up. There's no way of guaranteeing anything, but in this case, I would recommend looking elsewhere first.

3. Confirm if the parents have any of the common health issues found in huskies

Certain hereditary health issues can be passed down to the litter. It's important to check with the breeder if the mother or father suffers from the following health issues:

- Cataracts
- Hip or Elbow Dysplasia
- Corneal dystrophy
- Progressive Retinal Atrophy
- Hypothyroidism
- Zinc Deficiency (very common in huskies)

Ideally, you want the parents to have as little previous health issues as possible, preferably none. Whether this affects your decision is entirely up to you, but you will need to be aware of it, for the future health of your husky puppy.

These health issues are so common that you may struggle to find a set of husky parents that do not have at least one issue. Cataracts alone affect at least 10% of the entire Siberian husky breed; you can now imagine how hard it will be to find both parents with no health issues.

4. Are you able to see the puppies with their mother?

It's unlikely the father will be available, but it's very important for you to see the litter with their mother. Watch their interactions closely; is the mother caring or aggressive to the litter? You can see which puppies out of the litter are hyper or calm? Who tried to interact with the mother more? Watch to see if the mother singles out any particular puppy.

You can learn a lot of behavioral traits from a moment like this. By paying close attention to social interactions and how the puppies interact with their mother, you can often get a clue as to how they will be when they're older. In just a short space of time you may see behavior that indicates certain tendencies. Did you notice any puppy to be particularly needy, timid, independent, boisterous, calm, or hyper?

5. Are the puppies weaned?

Puppies should be weaned off their mother's milk at around seven weeks old. If they are not, it may be a sign that something isn't quite right, and you'll have to ask why this is the case.

If you're looking at puppies that aren't yet weaned, it could suggest health issues or more than likely they are in fact younger than 7 weeks old. If age is the issue, it leads to further concerns. Why is the breeder trying to sell their puppies under 8 weeks old? You'll have to ask some more questions and be very careful with how you proceed. Aside from state laws, 8 weeks old is the industry standard and any **reputable** breeder will stick to the rules, especially when the puppy's health is at stake.

6. Are you seeing the full litter?

The average litter size for Siberian huskies is between 4 and 6, although in some rarer cases it may be under 4, or over 6.

It's important to know if you are able to see the entire litter and ask if you can pick them up. By handling a few of the husky puppies you can get a sense of their size, character, and health. Is there one that's particularly smaller than the rest? Is there a runt? You can also get a small insight into their temperament when you pick them up, do they go to nip you? Show any aggression or frustration, or are they instantly calm and receptive to you?

This will all go towards helping you choose your ideal pup.

When it comes to runts of the litter, many people are unsure whether it's ok to pick them. The short answer is yes it is ok. But, you must perform some extra health checks and ask the breeder further questions. Although runts come out much smaller and weaker than the rest, it does not mean they can't go on to live a normal happy life like any other puppy. In fact, contrary to common belief, runts, if given the proper care will actually grow back to nearly their full "normal" size within a year or two.

The health and condition of the runt will come down to the care he had received right after being born. Oftentimes the runt will be too weak amongst the other puppies and will usually miss out on valuable feeding times from the mother. This is why it's essential for breeders to step in right away to ensure the runt is receiving everything he needs. It's important for you to refer to health tests that the breeder should have had done, and ask the breeder what kind of help they gave to the runt when he was born. Runts, can go on to live normal lives, but there is always an increased chance of health issues. It's important to know before making a decision

7. What stage are the puppies at with vaccinations?

It's really important to know what stage the puppies are at with vaccinations. Typically, puppies are vaccinated anywhere between 6-9 weeks, and then again at 10-12 weeks.

If you are taking your puppy home at 8 weeks old it's entirely possible he has not yet started his vaccinations. In which case, you'll be required to get both sets done.

General health guidelines state that you shouldn't take your puppy outside until 2 weeks after his second set of vaccinations. This ensures he is strong and healthy enough to combat any exposure to nasty bacteria that could be in your yard or Local Park; more on this topic later.

8. Have the puppies received any other treatments, such as worming?

Fun fact: All puppies are born with worms! So it's important that all puppies receive some on-going worm treatment. Usually, worming treatment starts at 2 weeks of age and repeats every 2 weeks until they're 12 weeks old. You need to confirm with your breeder that the puppies have already started their worming treatment and how long they have left. It's also a good idea to ask if they will give you the rest of the treatment or if you have to buy your own.

9. Can the breeder provide references from other previous buyers

You shouldn't feel awkward or rude asking this question. Any good breeder will understand and even expect you to verify them. The most reliable way to do this is from previous buyers. Previous buyers can tell you about how their puppy has developed and any information about the breeder that will help you.

Your breeder may have their own references, but of course, this opens up the possibility of them picking and choosing people who they know will say only good things. Another way is to visit your local veterinarian as they may have some more unbiased reviews about the breeder.

Good breeders will be known by the local veterinarian practices, and breeders who are shady, may not be known by them at all. This is another good way to tell apart reputable breeders from illegitimate ones.

10. Is the puppy registered with the Kennel Club?

If you are looking to buy a pedigree Siberian husky puppy, it's important that your breeder has registered him with the Kennel Club within your country. Getting puppies registered can take a while, but your breeder should have already started the application process. In the case that the puppy's application is pending, you should be able to see certification that both parents are pedigree.

11. What food are the puppies eating right now? Can you take home a diet sheet?

In the very beginning, it's a great idea to continue feeding your puppy the same food he's on while with the breeder. I'll explain why later, for now, be sure to ask the breeder what type of food the puppies are eating, what time they have their meals and if you can take home a handy diet sheet with all of that information on it!

Some of the breeders I've visited in the past have even given me a small amount of their puppy food, just to help me out until I'm able to go and buy my own bag of it. Your breeder may not do this, but it's definitely worth asking!

12. Are you able to return your puppy if you discover a serious health problem?

I hope this kind of situation doesn't happen to you, but it's more common than you may think. It's very important to confirm whether or not the breeder will accept you returning the puppy upon discovering serious health issues that can't be managed. *(Within reasonable time)*

It's up to you, of course, if you want to commit to an unhealthy puppy from the beginning. There's nothing wrong with doing that, so long as you are aware of the difficulty to follow. An unhealthy puppy will require a lot of treatment and trips to the vet. All of which will come with a lot of stress and large vet bills.

13. Is there a contract of sale?

Contracts are important for many things in life, and it's no different for when you purchase a puppy. All reputable breeders will provide a contract of sale that will state the responsibilities of both the breeder and the owner. It will state any other important information that you both agree on. This will also act as an official document that you can keep.

Huskies From Around the World

This is Nanuk. He finally made it to the family of his dreams. He's loving life on the Gold Coast, Australia. He's 6 years old.

MEET *Nanuk*

6 YEARS, FROM GOLD COAST, AUSTRALIA!

Husky Puppy Supplies List

To make your life easy when you bring your new puppy home, you'll want to have a complete list of supplies ready to go. There's nothing worse than continuously realizing you need different items, at different times, which you kept forgetting to buy. So here's your complete list of essentials.

Saving money is always a priority for most of us, and dog supplies aren't always cheap. In the long run, you'll likely end up spending a fair amount on your husky and it's to be expected. For some products, it's ok to opt for a "cheap" version, but for others, you'll only want to choose a reputable brand. When buying items like toys, which your pup will be putting in his mouth, it's better to go for a reliable brand. Many "cheap" versions of well-known toys aren't made as well, and can oftentimes break, causing choking hazards. Fortunately, if you use an online store like Amazon to get your supplies, there are many customer reviews that you can check before making a purchase.

After speaking with countless owners about how much they spend on their dogs, it seems most of them report saving money in the long run when they buy their supplies online, Amazon as it happens, is their go-to store. You can also take advantage of sales and discounts more frequently online, than from your local brick and mortar stores.

Your complete husky pup supply list:

1. Standard wire crate.

I recommend getting a crate size of 42 inches. At first glance you may think this is big for a puppy, but in my experience, it actually isn't. I wouldn't recommend anything bigger than this, but if you wanted to opt for smaller that's ok, although it may not last for when he's grown.

One thing to mention, in the beginning, it's preferable to have a crate in your bedroom for sleeping as well as one downstairs throughout the day. If you don't mind carrying the crate then getting one will be ok, but if that proves to be too difficult, you'll need to get two crates.

What to look for in a crate:

- Double doors for easier in and out training.
- Double latches as huskies love trying to escape.
- Slide-out bottoms for easy cleaning.
- Dividers. Can reduce the size of the crate inside.
- Easy fold down and carry handle for moving around your house. In the beginning, you'll need to have your crate in your bedroom for sleeping, and downstairs during the daytime for general training.

I personally don't recommend any other type of crate. The other types would be fashion crates or wooden crates, canvas crates or heavy duty crates. In one way or another, these crates all have more flaws than the standard wire crate. As crates are not the cheapest item to buy, I recommend getting one that won't break or needs to be replaced; exactly what happens with the other types.

2. Metal food and water bowls.

All you need are some simple metal bowls for his mealtimes and water. It's best to go for stainless steel options as he will be less inclined to chew it. Plastic bowls get destroyed quickly.

3. Puppy food

If you're lucky enough, your breeder will give you a small amount of food to take home when you get your puppy. I recommend using it as it will give your puppy a sense of familiarity while in his new surroundings. Don't forget that you will still need your own supply of food from the store, so even if your breeder offers you theirs, remember to pick some up some extra.

Diet is a very big topic with a lot of strong opinions behind it. Whether you should feed your puppy commercial dog food or follow a raw food diet is something I will cover later on. I'll lay everything out for you to make your own decision.

4. Leash, collar, and harness.

Although you won't be taking your pup down the park for quite some time, it's important to get yourself a basic leash, collar, and, harness for a couple of reasons. For one, it will come in handy when you implement some potty training, which will happen from the first day home. And secondly, leash training can come way before he's allowed to go outside, so it's best to have it all ready.

5. Puppy bed

It's tempting to get a fancy soft bed for your puppy but this isn't a particularly good idea. When the teething process starts, your puppy's soft bed will be one of his first victims. You can avoid this by instead opting for a water-resistant one. These beds are less enticing to chew as they're made from a tougher material but still designed to be comfortable. A water-resistant bed will also prove much easier to clean when your pup makes a few potty mistakes *(which will definitely happen!)*

6. Puppy gate or baby gate

Creating boundaries and keeping your puppy in limited areas of your house is super important for training, which I'll cover later on. The way you do this is with puppy gates or baby gates. They both work great and you may already have a baby gate at home. I really suggest using one at least 3ft high; Huskies are strong and soon learn to jump high. You could just opt to shut the doors of each room all of the time, but it's nicer to use a gate; it will allow you and your pup to see each other from other rooms. In my opinion, this is much better and will help your pup remain comfortable when you want him to remain in "his" area.

7. Brush

Brushing your husky will prove to be more important as he grows a little older. Puppies, in general, don't require much brushing and their coat is still thin and their skin is fragile. The best type of brush for a puppy is a Pin & Bristle combination brush. Pin brushes are made from thin pins with small plastic balls on the end. The smooth rounded balls ensure your puppy's skin doesn't get scratched. Bristle brushes (like a toothbrush) are soft brushes that are great for finishing off your grooming session. This is the ideal brush for your puppy and they're relatively cheap. You may not be doing much brushing to begin with, but it's still a necessary purchase.

8. Different style of toys

There are many different types of toys out there and it's essential to arm yourself with a few of them. The varying styles are made for different reasons.

- **High-value training toys:** These are toys that you don't often let your puppy play with and are used for training purposes. As he won't get to play with that toy very often, he'll consider it to be of high-value. This will significantly improve his response to your commands and will help your training efforts be more successful. Soft teddy bears make ideal training toys

- **Durable toys:** These are generic, hard-wearing toys that you can leave down for your puppy to chew on. These are usually hard plastic/rubber toys and will be essential for when your puppy starts teething. The Kong toy is a good example of a standard long-lasting chew toy.

- **Dog bones:** These are known for their durability and they can often last a long time. Your puppy will taste a slight flavor to keep him attracted to it and they prove to be significantly more appealing than a standard rubber/plastic chew toy.

- **Interactive/puzzle toys**: These will keep your puppy entertained for lengthy periods of time and are useful when you need to get on with your own things. Interactive toys will encourage your puppy to use his brain and they provide valuable mental stimulation. Mental stimulation is often overlooked and it has a bigger impact on your puppy's general behavior than you think. I'll have a section on mental stimulation later on in the book.

9. Puppy treats

Having a range of treats at your disposal is extremely important and shouldn't be undervalued. In the early months when puppies are still in the communication building stage, you have to rely heavily on treats to keep their attention on you. Under 4 months of age, your puppy doesn't really understand that they need to listen to you, so that's why treats are so necessary. As your puppy grows and understands your voice and commands you can use treats a little less, and praise him with your tone of voice or with toys. For now aim to have a range of tasty treats ready to go.

The best types of treats to have:

- Very small nibbles. As you're going to need to use a lot of treats throughout training exercises, you have to keep the treats very small, so you don't impact his overall caloric intake for the day *(too much)*.

- Real pieces of cooked turkey or chicken make an ideal treat.

- Tiny clumps of peanut butter work like a charm. Use a salt free or limited salt option as well as one that only uses natural ingredients.

- If you opt for store-bought treats, try to go for one that's made for puppies, limited in its ingredients, and always check the reviews first.

- If you're puppy LOVES his mealtimes, there's nothing stopping you using his dry kibble as a treat too. Dry kibble is also very small, perfect for portion control.

10. Poop scoop, bags, and special garbage bin

Your life will contain a lot of extra poop in it, once you get a puppy. So ensure you get a hard plastic poop scoop with a smooth surface for easy cleaning. It's important to get special bags and a separate garbage bin just for the waste. Remember, you can't put poop with household waste, as it needs to be disposed of differently.

11. Spare towels

Having plenty of old spare towels will make your life a lot easier! Have these close to hand in the same area that your puppy spends most of his time. You'll be amazed at the amount of mess some puppies make. Nothing beats having quick-access cleaning towels to put down when your pup spills his water bowl, vomits, pees, or creates any mess.

12. ID Tags for his collar, harness

When you start taking your pup outside, it's crucial to have an ID tag on his harness. The tag should have multiple phone numbers and your home address with a zip code. If your puppy is chipped then this should also be indicated on the tag. It does help to have your puppy's name on the tag, but this should not replace the space for the essential information

13. First aid kit

Accidents happen and in moments of panic, nothing beats knowing exactly where your first aid kit is. This is often forgotten about and that's understandable too, accidents don't happen much and we also don't anticipate them. But, even though you may never need to use it, you should have one. Pet first aid kits are so similar to human first aid kits that you don't need to specifically buy a "pet" one. If you already have a restocked human first aid kit, this will be just fine.

14. Bitter apple spray / Apple cider vinegar spray (DIY) version

You might not have heard of this one. Bitter apple spray is a solution that you can spray onto items that you don't want your puppy to chew or bite. It contains ingredients that *nearly* all puppies hate. Aside from actual bite inhibition training, sprays like this are very handy to have and I do recommend getting some. Remember, puppies aren't born knowing what they are and are not allowed to bite. You may just save your expensive sofa or furniture legs if you spray them before your puppy roams around the room.

You can make your own solution by using 2 cups of apple cider vinegar solution with 1 cup of regular white vinegar. This will be an effective homemade version.

Always test solutions first on an unseen patch of your sofa or furniture. In rare cases, it may react and discolor. Test first!

15. Pet-safe cleaning products

You may already have plenty of cleaning products, but your standard household bleach is really toxic for your puppy. It's important that you stock up on some pet-safe cleaning products for when your puppy makes a mess. Brands that produce pet-safe cleaning products include Puracy, Natures Miracle, Mrs. Meyer's, PetSimplicity, SpotAway, and Seventh Generation. You can find these on Amazon or your local pet store will have a range of pet-safe options.

16. Food container

Keep your puppy's food fresh and tasting great by having it kept in an air-tight container. Puppy food comes in big plastic bags and once you open them, it's hard to keep the food fresh unless you transfer it to a large air-tight container.

This list should do for now! You may already have some of the items and if not, you know what to look for.

Huskies From Around the World

This is Zoe Belle. She's 11 weeks old and looking gorgeous!
She's from Naperville, Illinois in the United Sates.

Preparing Your House

After you've gathered all of the necessary supplies your pup will need, It's time to puppy-proof your house. Preparing your house for your pup's arrival is an important thing to do for their health and safety. Trust me, his curiosity will have him searching nooks and crannies you never knew existed.

The best way to make all of your rooms safe is to think about your house from your puppy's perspective. He'll be down on the floor where his tiny nose can reach very small places. Ask yourself, what's going on down low in your rug? Where can he stick his nose and will it be a problem?

Below I will cover as many things that I'm aware of, to help you make your home safe and as puppy-ready as it can be.

House preparation list:

1. Electric cables and wires

Electric cables are very dangerous for your pup, especially throughout his teething period where he'll want to chew everything he can. A nice, soft plastic cable seems like the perfect texture to chew on. It may be, but it could be life-threatening.

I like to go through room by room and look for existing electric cables that are dangling or loose on the floor. Cables from lamps or your TV are good examples. The best thing you can do is use small cable-clips to tack the cable right in the corner of your floor to your skirting. By having the cable tucked right in the corner, your pup won't be physically able to chew it.

I know this seems like overkill, but don't underestimate your pup's curiosity. I strongly suggest spending an afternoon ensuring your cables are in a safe place.

2. Phone chargers

Yep, this is kind of the same as No.1 but I want to give it distinct recognition. Think about how normal it is to use your phone while it's plugged in, then as you leave, you simply pull out the cable and drop it down as you walk away. It's so easy to forget that your charger poses serious threat to any overly curious puppy. You must be extra conscious when moving around your charger from plug to plug, leaving it in areas where your puppy may be able to access it.

3. Puppy gates

The first item to put to use from your supply list will be puppy gates or baby gates. These will be needed for training purposes, and for safety.

When you bring your pup home, you don't want him to have free roam of your house, despite how tempting it is to let him run wherever he likes. Your puppy needs to know his boundaries early on; and only allowing him in a certain area of your house is the first step that lets him know he's not in charge, which proves very important for training purposes. I'll cover more on this later.

You'll also need to have gates in place to keep your puppy safe when you need to take your attention away from him. You can't focus on your puppy every second of the day, although that would be lovely, I'm sure you have things to do! Being able to confine your puppy in a set area you know he's safe in, is very valuable and you'll need to do it many times.

4. Designated daytime area

Before your puppy comes home, it's good to have in mind a set place he'll be during the day. This all depends on your house and the rooms you have, but in most houses, the kitchen or dining room usually seems to be the best choice. Whatever room you choose, it's ideal if it has hard floors, so if your puppy catches you off guard and makes a potty mistake, it will be much easier to clean up.

The designated space should contain his crate, bed, food and water bowl and some toys. Have spare towels and pet-safe cleaning products in close proximity. I have a complete section on setting boundaries later on which will dive in deeper about your pup's daytime area and why it's so important.

5. Designated sleeping area

The best place for your pup to sleep will be in a crate, besides your bed. When your puppy leaves his mother and siblings it can be very daunting and overwhelming. This usually makes sleeping a challenge, at least in the beginning. Your puppy will have an easier time sleeping if he knows he's near to you. Equip his crate with nothing more than a waterproof bed and a comforter which can be an old t shirt, some material from your breeder or a snuggle-puppy toy. While he's less than 4 months of age, he won't be strong enough to rip up or chew through the material.

Having a crate in your bedroom and downstairs during the day can be a pain. It means you have to get two crates or move a single one around. As crates are not that cheap you may want to buy just one. But this is completely up to you. The crate I suggest is a standard wire crate, which usually has carry handles and is not *too* heavy.

6. Designated potty training area

Upon bringing your puppy home, he'll need to eliminate right away and then almost every hour there on after. As you'll find out quite soon, potty training begins immediately, so in preparation, you'll need to make a designated pee and poop area for your pup. This area should be fairly small, away from the main focus of your yard with limited distractions nearby. This will be where you train him to pee and poop so ensure it's a place of your yard you don't mind sacrificing. If you don't have a front or back yard at all, you'll have to do the same thing but inside your house. In this case, it would be a good idea to purchase a potty pad. Please do not use a potty pad if you do have access to an outside yard. That will all be discussed in the training segment.

7. Indoor trash cans

It's really easy to forget this one. It's likely you have small trash cans in different rooms of your house, including your living room, bedroom, and dining room, too. Most of the time these are made out of plastic, or some kind of wicker or even leather to match your furnishings. Unfortunately these trash cans fall prey to your new excitable pup, and he'll love nothing more than to rummage through them, and even drag them around your house! I strongly suggest removing them or changing them for a heavier, taller trash can that your pup can't knock over or jump inside. Many years ago, I thought I had lost my puppy, only to discover a weird ruffling noise at the bottom of a plastic trash can in my living room. What made it even funnier is that he managed to avoid making any mess as he jumped inside, so I had no idea he was in the trashcan until it started moving. After lifting up newspaper and banana peels I found him staring back up at me with his tail wagging, glee on his face and garbage in his mouth. I changed all the bins the next day. That also got me using puppy gates and keeping him in set areas when I left the room.

8. Final check of the floors and all nooks & crannies

Like I mentioned already, your pup's curiosity is literally never-ending. Anything that you don't pick up from your floor, your puppy will find it and inspect it. Just like with babies, it's so important to remove any accessible choking hazards. Your puppy is young, and he isn't aware of things he can and can't chew, or whether or not it will choke him, so we have to manage that situation ourselves.

It's great to have this done before your puppy arrives but just know that puppy-proofing your home will be a never-ending process. As days and weeks go past your home will change dramatically in ways you may not be aware of. You should always check your floors for new things your puppy may try to chew and eat. It may save you an unwanted trip to the vet!

Huskies From Around the World

This is the beautiful Harper Nicole.
She's from the United States and is 4 years old!

Setting Boundaries for Your Puppy

I mentioned earlier how important it is to set boundaries, and how it's a good idea to have puppy gates and create designated areas.

So you may be wondering what all the fuss is about "why can't I just put my puppy down in the living room and let him be, I'll still watch him" well, you can still do that, especially in the evening times when you want to encourage some bonding. But it's not a good idea to give him a free roam of your house, *all the time*. This complete freedom to go where he wants can encourage your pup to think he's the boss, and if this happens, he won't have good reason to listen to you. This will make training really difficult.

It's easy to get lost in all of your excitement; after all, you have a new husky puppy! but remember, having a good system and habits in place from the start will make your life so much easier, and your husky will actually be much happier if he's guided, and knows his place in your family.

Setting boundaries and limiting your puppy to certain rooms of your house is the easiest way to establish the correct hierarchy in your family. It shows your pup that you and your family members are "higher in the pack" than he is, as he isn't allowed in all the areas that you are. Dogs, in general, are social animals and have a strong hierarchical system ingrained into them. This means that they listen, follow, obey and respect the pack leader, or anyone that's above them. When you bring your new pup home, you have to make sure he knows that you are the pack leader, and at the very least, higher in rank than him. If your puppy thinks he's in charge or he has an unclear understanding of who else is in charge, he just isn't going to listen to you. This will make things a lot harder from the beginning.

At the same time, I don't want to sound like your puppy is a new recruit to your army training facility! It's so important that your puppy feels a part of the family too, so setting boundaries doesn't mean confine him to a single room 24/7. It's more about limiting him throughout the day, until you have certain moments, in the evening when you and your family are watching TV and you can all bond together. There's nothing more enjoyable than spending some quality time with your fluff ball after long day.

It's important to remember that you're doing this for good reason, you're not being mean or unfair, and it's simply setting the correct standards for your husky to understand. He should know what his primary room is, and that he only gets to go in the living room or upstairs when you (the pack leader) let him. It's almost like training him before you even start training him!

On top of all the valuable training benefits, it also helps you to keep him safe. As much as you're going to try, it's hard to pay attention to your puppy all of the time and you're going to need to go upstairs, eventually leave the house and run errands... So having a set room from the beginning will make it easier for moments when you can't watch him, you'll know he's safe in *his* room.

In his designated daytime area, you can have his crate, some durable chew toys, food and water bowl, his bed, poop bags, spare towels and cleaning equipment close to hand. Aside from puppy-proofing your whole house like we discussed in the previous section, you can consider this room to be the *ultra*-puppy-proofed area that he can remain safe in no matter what.

Once again, I just want to clarify that setting boundaries is a way for you to have an even closer and stronger relationship with your pup, not a more distant one. Adult huskies or any dog for that matter will have a much tighter bond with their owners than those dogs who did not receive the correct lessons and guidance in the beginning.

For canines, setting boundaries is the beginning of establishing respect, and establishing respect is the beginning of all amazing relationships.

Huskies From Around the World

This is Hanna, after being born in Slovakia,
She then moved to Spain where this photo was taken.
She's 6 months old and looks amazing!

MEET *Hanna*
6 MONTHS, FROM SLOVAKIA!

Getting Your Puppy to Sleep

Getting your pup to sleep can be just as difficult as it is with a new born baby. In fact, it's not uncommon for your puppy to be around 4 months old before he's sleeping throughout the whole night.

Fortunately, there are many things that you can do to make the sleeping issue, well, not really an issue at all. With a few tips and tricks and some easy bedtime routines your puppy's sleep will be better than yours! Of course, there's going to be some hiccups along the way, but after all, he's still a puppy!

This section will touch on some information you need to know about your puppy and his crate, but not all. Getting your puppy comfortable in his crate, as well as knowing what to do when your puppy cries in his crate, will both be left until the crate training section.

Where should your puppy sleep?

When it comes to your puppy's sleeping arrangements, the first thing to establish is where your puppy should sleep.

While some people prefer different setups, the one that seems to be the most successful across the board, is having your puppy sleep in a crate, in your bedroom near to your bed.

Aside from potty breaks, one of the main reasons your puppy will wake up during the night is because he won't be able to sense his mother beside him. Dealing with this separation is difficult for any puppy and being in a completely new environment only adds to it. Potty breaks and missing his mom, will lead to a few restless nights.

The best way for you to manage this is by locating his crate next to your bed. He will be able to sense that you are close to him throughout the night which will provide valuable comfort. It definitely trumps leaving him alone downstairs in your kitchen. You may not exactly be his canine parent, but you are now his human one and that more than counts!

Are you thinking about having your pup sleep with you in the bed?

I know how wonderful it seems to cuddle up to your cute puppy in bed, but it is not a good idea. As your puppy is young and not yet potty trained, it's best to teach him that when night time arrives, he goes to his bed, and you go to your bed. There will be many potty mistakes in the beginning and the last thing you want is for your puppy to pee or poop on your bed. Despite the cuteness, this just isn't hygienic enough!

It would also lead your puppy to believe that your bed is now his bed, right from the first time, and his crate from then on would become a downgrade and even considered a punishment. This would cause a problem for the next time you do actually need to put him in his crate.

Although I too love the idea of having puppies and dogs sleeping with us in the bed, I don't think it's a good idea, and I personally recommend that you keep your bed as your sleeping area and not your pup's

Establishing a bedtime routine

For your puppy to have a good sleep, you must establish a good bedtime routine and stick to it on a nightly basis.

As you get further into the evening and closer to bedtime, you have to start thinking about your puppy's sleep. Let's run through a good bedtime routine that you can follow below:

1. **Make his last meal and drink at least 2-3 hours before bedtime.** Your puppy should not eat or drink anything for at least 2-3 hours before going to sleep and this includes eating treats. This time period helps your pup properly digest his food before going to sleep. It also avoids having an excess of energy throughout the night. After your pup finishes his last meal, guide him directly outside to eliminate.

2. **Burn some final energy.** Allow 45 minutes for his last meal to digest, and then encourage him to play. Throw his toys, play some gentle tug of war, throw the ball and have him running around your house. The goal here is fairly simple; expel as much energy as you can as bedtime approaches. This works wonders at using up some of his final energy; but be sure to have a period for him to calm down before he goes to his crate. When you stop playing with him, lead him directly outside for another potty break, as he will likely need to go.

3. **Dim the lights and lower the volume.** Do this after your playtime session. This won't just help you sleep better; it will help your puppy too! As you approach bedtime, you should turn the bright lights off and if you're watching TV or talking, lower the volume a little. This creates a more calming environment with less stimulation. Try doing this for 30 minutes before you intend on taking him to bed.

4. **Final potty break.** The final and most important step. Before your pup goes to sleep, take him out for one last trip to the potty spot. If at first, he seems like he doesn't need to go, stick it out for 5 minutes or more. Use your go-to potty command like "potty-time" and encourage him to pee or poop. Avoid all distractions and other communication with your pup. If after a good 5 minutes he's still not showing any interest in going, it's time to sleep.

By following these steps, you're giving your pup an incredible chance of having a great sleep. You're meeting all of his needs; he's fed, he's received some bonding time and your attention; he's been let out to eliminate multiple times and he's also had a chance to calm down and relax in a less stimulating environment ready for bed time, which happens to be right next to you while you sleep too. It's crucial that you're confident with your bedtime routine, as you'll be much better prepared for when he cries throughout the night, as I will discuss in more detail, later on.

What to put inside your puppy's crate?

Pimping out your puppy's sleeping crate is not entirely necessary or best practice. In the past I have seen some overly-decorated crates, *to say the least*. I'm not one for judging the decision of others, but I'll just say this; I once saw a framed painting of a beach, hanging on the inside of the crate, next to an actual clock. And it was ticking.

I honestly, have no idea what that was all about, and I didn't ask. But all I know, Is that it probably *wasn't* necessary. And dogs can't tell the time...

Back to it! I recommend having very limited items inside the crate and I'll go through them below:

- **Puppy bed or waterproof mat.** The main thing to have in his crate is a bed/waterproof mat. It's also important to keep a section of hard floor accessible inside the crate, in case your puppy wakes up and eliminates without crying. Naturally, puppies don't like to soil where they sleep but he'll have no choice if there isn't a section of hard floor available.

- **One soft comforter item.** A comforter could be something like a snuggle puppy toy, which by the way are great! But these are a tad on the expensive side and you can give your puppy something else that you have plenty of, used t-shirts.

Before you wash your t-shirt, put it in your puppy's crate when he goes to sleep. By snuggling up to an old t-shirt of yours, he will feel like you're there with him throughout the night. The sense of smell is very powerful for all puppies, and this trick works well. Of course, you have to be happy to sacrifice a t-shirt, it may end up a little chewed or worse, pooped on. One soft comfort item is enough though, never overload his crate. *Or hang artwork.*

- **Try a blanket over the crate.** By putting a blanket over the crate, it may allow your puppy to feel more safe and secure. However, this isn't preferred by all puppies and he may not like it. See how he reacts when you have the blanket on the crate, and when you have it off the crate. The biggest giveaway will be how easily he enters. If he's comfortable with the blanket option, he won't have any issues going in, but if he's intimidated by the blanket, he'll resist getting in his crate.

Following the tips and advice above will definitely help your pup have a good sleep. But remember, it won't happen overnight (excuse the pun). In the beginning, it will be difficult, but as your puppy feels more comfortable with you, his environment, and his bedtime routine, better sleep isn't too far away!

Dealing with potty issues throughout the night

Your cute little husky pup is still very small, which means his bladder, is also still very small. So small in fact, during the daytime he'll probably need to pee or poop almost every hour. So, how on earth will he last throughout the night? The answer is quite simple, he won't!

Fortunately, during sleep, your pup won't need to eliminate *as* much, but without a doubt, you'll need to take him out and you should do, at least once throughout the night.

So, when should you take him out?

In the very beginning, you should see how your puppy reacts, does he cry to be let out? Or does he stay quiet and pee inside his crate without you knowing. Usually, it will be the former. Puppies instinctively don't like soiling their crate so they are more likely to start crying. This is the only time I'll suggest responding to cries, (more on that later) for now, you need to let your puppy out, so take note of the time that he cries. Take him outside to his potty spot, wait until he goes, then head back inside and off to sleep again. It's important to take note of the time, because ideally, you don't want to make a habit of responding to your puppy's cries, this will lead to your demise! Instead, get a good idea of what time he usually cries, then set your alarm 15-20 minutes before, wake him up and take him out to potty. Going to potty is important and you cannot avoid it. But you ALWAYS want to manage and limit crying. In the beginning it's likely you'll have to directly respond to his cries, but as you'll find out later, this is not a good thing to do. If you're unsure on how the potty spot works, that will be covered completely in the potty training section below.

I will also cover how to deal with your puppy crying inside his crate. The situation above will be one of the reasons why he cries, and now you know how to deal with that. However, there are a couple of other scenarios that I will discuss later on, in the crate training section.

Huskies From Around the World

This is Blue. He's enjoying the good life in the Philippines! He's 3 months old here.

Exercise and Playtime

Siberian huskies are not short of energy, and if you haven't done any research on the breed already, you must know right now that you're about to become very fit. Their exercise requirements are so significant, it's often the topic that sways many people's decision on getting a husky or not.

Adult Husky Talk...

There's a lot of generic information out there in the online dogmosphere, and it just astonishes me that still to this day I see veterinarians recommend 1 hour of exercise per day **for a husky.** 1 hour of exercise per day is generic dog advice that's designed to "be ok" for all breeds. When there isn't a whole lot of specific information out there, I don't blame for you believing the generic advice, too. But for a Siberian husky, 1 hour is not ideal. Of course 1 hour is absolutely better than 0 hours, but **ideally** your husky should receive 2 hours of intense physical exercise per day, spread over a couple of sessions, 1 hour in the morning and 1 more hour in the evening.

Huskies are outdoor lovers and if you already aren't, I'm sure you will be soon. Go and explore new paths, trails, forests and hikes with your husky. There's nothing more beautiful than taking your Siberian out to discover new areas, watching his senses and instincts spark up like never before. Exercise will forever be his favorite moment of the day. If you give you him the physical activity he desires, I promise you, you'll never have any issues with him and he'll be a well-behaved, obedient husky.

It's so sad when something so critical to their health and behavior is neglected. I must have had by now hundreds of people ask me about why their husky is behaving in a certain way, destroying things, constantly hyper, anxious, the list goes on. And my first question is **always** about exercise; so much so that I even feel like I'm not trying with my response; but, the matter of fact is that 85% (an honest guestimation) of all of those issues stem from a lack of exercise. Of course I'm not disregarding other contributing factors and there are many, but in my experience exercise is nearly always it. A husky cannot go a day without exercise; dedicated exercise. If this happens throughout the week, and following months, you have to expect bad behavior, regardless of the training you've given. What's worse than bad behavior is the simple fact that your husky would no longer be happy.

Your puppy is a little different, though

Husky puppies are a little different. In fact, when you're dealing with a puppy, you can't exercise them as you would an adult husky. Their bones, joints, and ligaments are all still under serious development and **too much** exercise could damage them and affect proper growth. It's just like with us; a young child would not follow the same workout that an adult would typically do as it would be detrimental to their body and growth.

So, how much exercise is ideal for a puppy?

A good rule to follow that ensures you don't over-exercise your pup is the **5 minute per month rule**. Don't worry it's not actually 5 minutes per month… In fact, it's 5 minutes per day, per month of age he has. So starting from the age of 1 month, you should stick to 5 minutes of dedicated exercise per day until he's 2 months old, where you will then increase it to 10 minutes per day, until he's 3 months old and it becomes 15 minutes, etc.

Dedicated exercise.

Dedicated exercise is when you actually go through the process of clipping on your leash and harness and walking with your puppy; as opposed to your puppy generally playing around on the floor.

But remember, you can't take him outside in the beginning. You have to wait until 2 weeks after his second set of vaccinations, which will usually be when he's 14-16 weeks old, depending on when he started. As soon as you are able to take him outside, you should do. Your puppy will benefit greatly from his initial outdoor experiences; it will build his senses, provide important mental stimulation and prepare him for his activity-filled life! But before you are able to take him outside, walks around your house will be the answer.

While your puppy is young, dedicated exercise should mostly be focused on walking, with the occasional run. Your puppy receives enough physical stimulation from playing so it's not advised to go hard with his dedicated routine.

Exercise from playing.

Exercise from playing is also important and will happen whether you want it to or not! Husky pups are playful creatures and will bounce around for as long as they can.

It's a good idea to monitor how much your puppy plays. If he's non-stop jumping around, darting across the room and fetching toys, his 5 minutes will be almost completely unnecessary, right?

Well, not quite, it's still very important to get your puppy familiar with his leash and harness as early on as possible. He will eventually need to wear it every day, so prepare him from a young age when he'll be more accepting of it. Your life will be so much easier with routines, so try making his 5 minutes of dedicated exercise happen at a certain time every day, before he has worn himself out with playtime. You can treat this as a start to leash training.

Husky puppy growth timeline

- **0 - 6 months.** Your husky will be growing the quickest during this stage. Therefore, this will be when his bones and ligaments are the most fragile and extra caution must be taken. Ideally, you follow the 5 minutes per month rule until the age of 6 months.

- **6 months - 1 year.** This is when the growth will slow down a little and your husky will likely be at his full height by his first birthday. Just remember that further development of his joint and ligaments will still be happening, just at a slower pace. You can start exercising your husky a little more, but consider how active he has already been for the day.

- **1 Year to 2 Years.** A lot of the growing would have slowed down significantly by the time he's 1 but you would be surprised. Male huskies in particular can take up to 36 months before they're fully filled out. However, around 18 months would be safe to start exercising your husky as you would for the rest of his life. Before this moment, keep a close eye on how much exercise you're giving him and still be cautious with his joints and bones.

Tips for making playtime exciting and educational

I'm going to cover something that your puppy will love, playtime! However, this isn't about buying your pup a new toy and just handing it to him. Playtime can be much more effective and beneficial for your puppy if you really engage with him and be a part of the game. When done in a certain way, it can also be a fantastic way to start training him without *really* training him...

A while back, my friend shared some advice and showed me how she had started playing with her husky pup "Juno", since then I've never done it differently.

Before fetch, which has more working parts to it than you think, should come the old classic, tug of war. This is actually the basis for a lot of playtime antics.

While you're on the ground at his level, try sparking your puppy's excitement by wiggling one of his new toys around in front of him. Let him sniff it, grab it, bite it. Really get his excitement up and if he sometimes diverts his attention to you and jumps on you, it's ok (in the beginning). This is actually building great associations for your puppy, he's having a great time, and he will associate these positive feelings with you.

After you've tempted your puppy into some basic tug of war style play, suddenly stop and just hold it still, make the toy "boring" so to speak. He may let go naturally or with some verbal encouragement. When he does let go, give him some good praise and wiggle the toy again to ignite his excitement.

This is still playtime and you're not really running him through some strict training exercises, but the effect of this is great. You're actually setting strong foundations for "leave it" whilst you're playing with him.

Once your puppy understands the idea of letting go, you can take it a step further, by throwing the toy. As soon as your puppy runs after the toy and bites it, don't wait for him to bring it back. Chase it with him, and when he makes contact with the toy, you can grab it too, revert back to wiggling and then once again, stop the toy, make it boring, make him let go, and once he does, throw it again and chase it with him.

When your puppy masters this, you level it up to fetch. By now, your puppy will understand enough to chase the toy, bring it to you, and once you hold the toy still, he will already know to let go, so you can repeat the fun.

After watching my friend play with her husky this way, it changed the way I do too, it's like your puppy is receiving the benefits of a training routine when all you're really doing is playing. This beats giving your pup a new toy and leaving him to play with it on his own, hands down!

My friend's husky Juno is now an adult, and he's not only super obedient but he's the grandmaster of fetch. And not just when playing. He fetches various items and brings them directly to my friend and let's go without saying a word. When my friend is feeling particularly lazy (all the time), she says "Juno, where's my phone?" and Juno literally goes and searches the whole house for her phone, picks it's up and brings it to her. This never fails to amaze me.

I learned quickly that this is normal in their household… *sorry!* And luckily for her, this is now Juno's favorite game.

While I don't suggest using your husky as a tool to retrieve your own items, this method of playing sets the foundation for a really obedient and intelligent husky.

Huskies From Around the World

This is Nika looking gorgeous!
She's 3 years old and from the UK, England.

When can you take your puppy outside?

A wonderful moment in your puppy's life is when he's able to explore the big wide world. It's finally time to see your little fluff ball enjoy the outdoors like he's supposed to. But before you get too excited, it is necessary to cover some important points on this topic.

Let's talk about vaccinations.

When you can *supposedly* take your puppy outside comes with many different opinions. Some owners and vets insist that your puppy doesn't step foot outside of your home, even into your yard, until 2 weeks after his final set of vaccinations. By this time, your husky will be around 16 weeks old.

The other answer is that you can take your puppy out in your own private yard from when you have him home and that it's much safer than your local park, so you don't need to worry… **So what advice do you follow?**

The best of both worlds

I like the approach that respects both answers. While I do agree that you should avoid going to your Local Park and public areas until 16 weeks old, you will need to venture out into your yard way before this time for potty training. Most of the world's top dog trainers also prefer this approach, and take their puppies outside (only in their yard) way before 16 weeks old.

I don't suggest using your yard as a daytime chill-out spot or play area, but I do strongly suggest that you use your yard for potty training from the first day you get your puppy home.

If it wasn't for potty training, I would totally stick to the inside-only rule. Your puppy learns habits quickly and if you allow him to eliminate inside your home until 16 weeks old, this is what he'll learn to be correct. When he's finally "allowed" to go outside, of course you'll prefer him to poop and pee there. Although by this stage, you're asking your puppy to unlearn a well-formed habit that you taught him. This will be very confusing for your pup and he'll find it difficult to understand that his potty spot has changed.

The only true way to avoid your husky making potty mistakes throughout his life is to teach him from day one, that he only pees and poops *outside* the house.

What I suggest

I believe that you should take your puppy out into your yard for potty training purposes only, as long as you know it's safe and free from hazards, which I will cover further below.

A solid potty training routine will have you taking your pup outside to the same small designated spot several times a day. But only for peeing and pooping, don't let your puppy wander around inspecting everything, keep him on a leash, in his poop spot. Then head back inside.

When your pup has completed his second set of vaccines by two weeks, you can let your pup spend a lot more time in your entire yard and you can start taking him to your local park.

There are a couple of times that I would even avoid a private yard

If you have recently moved into your house, within the last 1-2 years and the previous owners had a dog. I would keep your husky pup inside until he's finished his vaccinations. There can be parts of your garden that may still contain harmful bacteria that the previous dog has left.

The other time it may be better to keep your pup inside is if your yard backs onto a public path where other dogs frequently walk down. If this is the case, your yard may contain similar bacteria that your park does and could make it risky for your pup.

Make your yard safe

Your puppy will take advantage of his newfound freedom in your yard, and you can bet he's going to sniff everything he can. However, your yard may contain any one of these common, yet hazardous items. It's really important to inspect your yard frequently to ensure your pup won't find the following:

- Lawn feed
- Mushrooms or fungi
- Toads or frogs
- Compost
- Fertilizer
- Acorns
- Conkers
- Weed killer
- Bulb plants (daffodils and lily)
- Bird food
- Snail or slug pellets
- Fruits that contain pits or stones
- Pesticides

Supervision is extremely important and even if you think your yard is hazard-free, you still shouldn't leave your pup unattended. On top of that, I understand that some of these items will be commonly used in your garden, especially if you are a keen gardener. In this case, I strongly recommend investing in a puppy pen. You'll be able to keep your puppy safe in here away from those hazards.

Be attentive to the weather

Your pup will be very sensitive to the weather while he's still young. In fact, your puppy won't even be able to regulate his own body temperature until he has his adult coat. This means it's your job to make sure he isn't exposed to conditions too hot or too cold.

It's true, huskies are one of the most resilient breeds we know of, but this comes later on in their life when they have the protection of their thick double layered coat. A fun fact: Siberian huskies can survive in temperatures as low as -50 degrees below zero, that's pretty impressive! But like I said, only when they're adults are they strong enough for all outside conditions.

Tips for when you take your husky pup to the park

It's an awesome moment when you can finally take your puppy out to explore the world like he's always wanted. I know you're itching to take him to the local park, so here are some valuable tips for when that moment comes.

- **Do a test run first.** For the first time your pup visits the park, go during a time that you know will be relatively quiet. Keep his first experience short and sweet. Be very attentive and watch his body language, is he happy to be in the park?

Does he look nervous, or scared? This will help you prepare for next time; your pup may need a series of short visits, before he starts feeling comfortable.

- **Be quick to ask other owners if their dog is puppy-friendly.** Don't worry about what they're going to think. You have every right to ask and you should do as well. Big dogs can easily cause injuries to young puppies. Keep your distance if the other owner restrains their dog, or says that they aren't particularly fond of puppies.

- **Be careful when taking treats.** Some parks may not even allow you to take dog treats or food in. Aside from that, it's wise keep your treats in a sealed bag in your pockets, not your hands. Treats can attract unwanted attention from other dogs, and things could get a little out of control. Only give treats to your pup, and be aware of other dogs around when you get them out of the bag.

- **Bring a bottle of water and a portable bowl.** Not all puppies can drink from water bottles, so it may be a good idea to invest in a small portable water bowl. These are often collapsible and can easily fit inside your pocket. It's very important to always have fresh cold water for your pup, and by having it in a bowl, it will be much easier for him to drink than from a bottle.

- **Always check your surroundings.** Your puppy will be having a blast, and so will you while you're watching him, but don't forget to constantly check your surroundings for other dogs and owners. Other dogs can be fast and come from nowhere, so always be attentive and ready to remove your pup from any unwanted situations.

- **Be cautious of other dogs, but not afraid!** By the time it comes to your local park ventures, ideally, you would have already started socializing your pup with other dogs beforehand (socialization is covered in the next section). So when there are other dogs at the park, you don't need to be afraid of letting your puppy interact with them. Interaction is a really important part of developing his social skills and mental capacity to handle new experiences. But, of course, do all that you can to make it safe, look at the other dog, their size, their body language, and even ask the owner if it's ok for your pup to go up to them.

- **Try to go off-leash as soon as possible.** If your puppy always comes to you when you call his name, it's best to let him off the leash when you enter the park (as long as it's not really busy). Why? Well, keeping your pup on the leash in a new environment can make him feel very vulnerable and this actually encourages negative confrontation from other dogs. **If your puppy doesn't yet come every time when called,** use a long leash, and let it drag behind him on the floor. This way you can still grab the leash if you need to.

- **Leave the park and try again if things aren't going well.** You may expect his first park experience to be amazing, but it's not always like that. There can be many reasons why your puppy doesn't enjoy his first park visit like you're anticipating. He may be intimidated being in a new area, or even worse you run into a large boisterous dog. The most important thing is to be attentive, and if your puppy isn't enjoying it, keep the visit short, leave, and return another day.

Remember that you don't have to rush anything. Keep your pup comfortable but always give him gentle encouragement. You can be waiting for the moment to take him to your local park with such excitement that it's easy to forget this can actually be fairly overwhelming for him.

Going back to the vaccination concern; I do think it's very important to use your yard as his potty training spot right from the first day home, and then give him full access to the outside once he has finished the vaccines. If you opt to keep your pup inside, that's entirely up to you, but it may prove rather difficult when you finally want to change his potty spot. I will cover this topic more in the potty training section later on.

Your puppy will be itching to explore the outside and it's a great moment when you can finally allow that. Keep the tips above in mind and you'll have a safe and pleasant experience to remember forever.

Huskies From Around the World

This is Dakota keeping it cool!
He's 3 years old, from California, USA

Socializing Your Puppy

Now we get to a very important part of raising a well-behaved, friendly husky puppy. Fortunately, Siberian huskies make friends easily and often do extremely well in any kind of social situation. So you already have a good start!

We can thank the Chukchi people from Eastern Siberia for the kind, friendly nature that the husky has today. The Chukchi's were a group of nomadic hunter-gatherers that originally bred Siberian huskies to help them with their lifestyle. Huskies were used primarily for transportation but occasionally helped with hunting and other generic tasks. But they weren't just working dogs, the Chukchi's considered their Siberian husky pack to be essential to their survival and well-being, therefore they treated the huskies as if they were family. This means the huskies slept with them in their tents, the tribe shared their food with the huskies, the huskies even played companionship roles and some stayed with the women while the men went out to hunt and travel. Treating the huskies in this way has made them the companionship-craving breed they are today AND they're extremely friendly with people, even strangers as well as other dogs.

Despite huskies having a great temperament when it comes to meeting new dogs and people, it's still important to practice socializing from a young age. **In fact, the recommended age to start socializing any puppy is 3-12 weeks old.** Most of you will pick up your pup at 8 weeks old, so you need to begin right away.

This can lead to a little bit of confusion... You may be thinking "how can I socialize my puppy this young, if I can't take him to the park until 16 weeks old?"

This is a great question and you're not alone, this is one of THE most asked puppy-related questions out there! Fortunately, the answer is easier than you think.

Although you shouldn't take your puppy to the local park before he has finished his vaccinations, **it doesn't mean he can't interact with other, clean, vaccinated dogs.**

5 ways you can socialize your pup without going to the park.

1. Take your pup to a friend's house. Meeting new people and being in a new environment will greatly improve his social skills by exposing him to some new "strangers". Your friend doesn't even need to have another dog, meeting new people works too.

2. Doggy play dates. If you know anyone with a healthy, vaccinated, puppy-friendly dog. Invite them over to your house, or visit their house. Even if that dog doesn't want to play with your pup, simply having them in close proximity will go towards positive social interactions.

3. Consider a puppy class. These are specifically made for puppy owners needing to socialize their pup, without going outside to the local park. There may be one in your local area, and you'll find out with a simple Google search. Or, if you have many friends all with puppies, you could even organize your own puppy class together in a nominated house. Note: some puppy classes are for training, and some are just for socialization purposes. You may even want to try both, but in my experience, the ones just for socializing are easier to get involved with.

4. Take your puppy out in a baby stroller. **Yep, believe it or not this is a thing.** Your pup can experience the outside world without having to step foot in any hazardous public areas. It's a fun option, but if you don't already have a stroller, I wouldn't recommend buying one just for this reason! They can be fairly expensive!

5. Take your pup out in short car journeys through your local area. He'll be able to see out the windows and smell the outside. Taking in the new environment even from the safety of your car, will start to spark your puppy's social desires. Be sure to have your puppy secured safely inside a crate, or on someone's lap.

The next one involves a park... my bad!

6. This kind of goes against the vaccination rule. But many people do it. You can decide if you would like to do this or not.

If you have any local parks where you know there ARE NOT many other dogs, you can take your puppy there; sit down with him on a blanket, inside a portable puppy pen. I know many people who do this and really enjoy it. Your puppy can watch the world go by and smell all the wonderful smells but in the safety of a nice blanket and pen. I can't stress enough the importance of going to a quiet spot. You want to avoid interaction with other dogs you know nothing about.

It's really important to try a few different options and keep consistent with your socialization sessions. Many professionals have found that with puppies, anything after 12 weeks old that they have not yet experienced, will be approached with greater caution. Fearfulness and anxiousness is commonly seen in dogs that did not receive enough socialization in their early weeks. This tends to show it's self in many situations that we would otherwise consider normal, like going to the park, having friends over or opening the door to the postman.

Although I mentioned above how huskies are naturally friendly, please don't assume your husky will be a complete saint when he's older. Regardless of his natural social abilities, you must engage in and maintain a good socialization routine from as young as possible.

One important thing to remember about socializing your puppy is that it's not ALWAYS about interaction with other dogs or people. Although that's the ultimate option, simply being in new environments counts. It's about experiencing different things and not just being confined to the same room and people on a daily basis. Socializing for us is about communicating with others, but for your puppy, it's much broader than this.

Be sure to make some Google searches on local puppy socialization classes. If you can make it to some of these, you won't regret it!

Huskies From Around the World

This is Leo with his amazing markings!
He's 3 months old from Rabat, Morocco

Choosing the Best Diet for Your Puppy

Choosing the diet that's most appropriate for you puppy can be a daunting task, especially with all the options and opinions about what's right and wrong. After this section you'll have your own plan of action and a lot less confusion. Before I start I'll say that getting your puppy's diet right may not happen on the first attempt, and as much as you want to limit changing foods, you may have to, hopefully just once, if at all. The main thing is to not worry, and you have plenty of time to find a food that works well for your pup. I'll first cover some important eating habits specific to huskies.

Many people consider huskies to be "fussy-eaters", and to some extent, this is true. But it's not *entirely* down to flavor preference. Siberian huskies in general, have fairly sensitive stomachs, so you have to remember this if you ever accidently assume he's just being fussy. The result of having a sensitive stomach means he may not get along with a lot of food brands or diet types, at least, to begin with. This would then cause him to refuse his food and it's easy to put it down to being fussy. There may be some element of fussiness, but the truth is that he will have an exceptional ability to know when his food isn't good for him, and if he's sensitive to it, he won't eat it.

A biological trait of huskies makes it easy to refuse food and go for long periods without eating. **What is it?** Behold their SUPER efficient metabolism, developed over thousands of years while they were bred by the Chukchi people in Siberia. Huskies need very little food for sustained energy, so if they don't feel like eating or it's even remotely uncomfortable, it's easy for them to go without.

So now you're at least aware of some difficulty you may face with your pup's diet and eating habits, let's get stuck into all the information you're going to need in order to keep your husky pup eating as he should.

What are the different diets?

When it comes to the different types of diet, there are only really two significant ones. You have the raw food diet and then a commercial dog food diet (dry kibble or wet food).

There's quite a bit of drama and strong opinions around what diet is best for your husky or husky puppy. Similar to all the various diets for us, there are pros and cons to all of them, some of them work better with different individuals and some don't. It will be the same for your husky too. It's always best to have an open mind about each diet and you may end up switching many times throughout your husky's life.

A brief summary of the raw food diet: What you need to know

The raw food diet is based on giving your husky raw meat, organs, ligaments, liver, bone, veggies, fruit and most include additional supplements to go alongside. Huskies are one of the world's oldest breeds, and you know for a fact that the Chukchi tribe wasn't going down to the local PetSmart 5000 years ago to pick up some dry kibble. So, this means that the raw food diet is what Siberian huskies would have eaten for thousands of years. This is one of the reasons why people believe it's better for a husky, to be eating like how they are used to. The second main reason is that it's much healthier than commercially made dog food. Raw food is "real" food and people swear that it's nutritionally better than any commercial store-bought option. Many experts do agree, but just as many disagree.

The difficulty with the raw food diet is that there are a lot of variables at play. There are specific ratios you must follow for how much meat you give compared to organs, compared to liver, bones, ligaments, veggies and fruits. On top of this, you must ensure the ingredients you're using are high quality, organic and sourced from a trusted location. Finally, it's hard to know what nutrients and how much of them are completely being absorbed by your husky's body, so this can lead to an imbalance of very important macro and micronutrients.

I personally do believe the raw food diet is very beneficial and "healthier" than a commercial kibble diet. <u>But it's not a diet that I would start my puppy off on.</u>

My opinion

Although I think a raw food diet is a healthier diet, I recommend sticking to a commercial puppy food based diet for at least the first year of your husky's life.

What you choose, is of course up to you, and this section is not about slamming one diet over the other. My best advice is to keep an open mind and think about how you want to raise your puppy. You may already have your mind up that a raw food diet is the way you want to go, and that's ok, but in that case, I strongly suggest getting professional help to set up the correct ratios, nutrients and food breakdown.

What I suggest

In the beginning, it's much easier and safer to stick to a commercial dog food diet. Feed your puppy 80% dry kibble with 20% wet food. Veterinarians recommend adding in wet food to provide varied nutrition; increase his water intake, as well as keeping it tasty and interesting with different textures.

As we are talking about huskies, I suggest a food that is made for dogs with sensitive stomachs; these are usually limited in their number of ingredients which make it easier to digest. They also avoid using common allergens and other undesirable ingredients.

Dog foods are always tailored to age. You can get a puppy, adult or senior dog food. You should only be getting the puppy dog food (both dry and wet). Each food contains different nutrients, vitamins, and minerals which provide extra support where it's needed, depending on age.

If you are just bringing your puppy home, ask your breeder what food they're using. Be sure to stick with that same food for at least a couple of weeks after coming home. If and when you want to change the food, you must do so gradually over the course of a 1-2 week period. Slowly adding in the new food and decreasing the old food, day by day. If you make a change faster than this, your puppy will suffer from an upset stomach, and your floors will suffer from diarrhea.

When to feed

When you first get your pup, it's a good idea to follow your breeder's advice as to how many times per day he should be fed. It can be an overwhelming experience for any puppy going to a new home, so the more you can help him feel comfortable, the better. Sticking to the same amount of mealtimes at the same time of day is one way to do this.

With puppies, it's nearly always 3 times per day, but some even have 4 meals. Whatever your breeder follows, you should stick to the same. What's also really important is the time of day. If your breeder had mealtimes at 7am, 2pm, and 6pm then you should follow that as well. If you no longer have contact with your breeder or you didn't have a breeder to begin with, stick to 3 times per day. Feed your pup when you wake up, a convenient time during the afternoon 12-3 pm and again in the evening, no later than 6 pm. (after 6 gets too close to bedtime and could disrupt his bedtime routine)

Once your pup reaches 6 months of age, it's usually best to switch to 2 times per day, once in the morning and again in the evening. Although before you do this, it's best to schedule a check-up with your vet to confirm this change.

When your pup reaches 1 year, you may consider switching your puppy food to an adult formula dog food. But once again, it's best to confirm this with your vet first to assess his health and overall development.

Portion size

Getting the portion size correct is a little trickier than you might have imagined. While there are guidelines on the packaging of the food (which is a good last resort) you shouldn't automatically use these values. After a visit to your veterinarian where they can professionally check your pup, they'll be able to guide you more accurately as to how much food *your* puppy needs. All pups are different and one specific amount of cups per day, isn't going to be fine for every puppy.

The correct portion size actually depends on a few factors one of them being the specific breed of your husky (Siberian Husky, Alaskan Husky, American Husky or Miniature Husky). These different breeds have different projected adult sizes, which changes the portion they should eat when they're puppies. Another factor that changes the portion size is actually the nutritional breakdown of the food itself. One cup of dry kibble from one brand may have a different amount of calories in it compared to another brand.

The absolute best way to determine the correct portion size is by visiting your veterinarian. Before you do this, stick to what your breeder is doing and then adjust it, once you're able to visit your vet. If you've adopted your husky pup, again, you're going to need to take him to the vets to have a health checkup and here you can clarify how much food he should have per day. Until you're able to find out from your vet, I recommend sticking to advice on the packaging of the food.

The packaging advice will base the portion size on your puppy's current age and weight. This is a safe guideline to use before visiting your vet.

Recommended options

With all the many options out there it can be hard knowing which food you should go for. Some brands do a better job than others, and when your pup's health is on the line, it's important to choose wisely.

Before getting into specific food, it's good to know of a website called the Dog Food Advisor. This website is literally a huge database of all the dog food and well-known brands on the market. They give a fair and unbiased analysis of not only each brand but nearly all of the brand's products as well. It has all the up to date information on recalled dog food, any toxic ingredients found in dog food, and provides an overall rating that you can feel confident using to choose a dog food.

It's important to note that over time, brands can change and formulas change too.

At the time of writing this book, some of the best dog food for puppies with sensitive stomachs is as follows below. All have been approved by the Dog Food Advisor already.

I recommend these four dry food options:

1. Nutro Ultra Superfood Puppy Dry Dog Food.

2. Blue Buffalo Wilderness High Protein Grain Free Natural Puppy Dry Dog Food.

3. Wellness Complete Health Natural Grain-Free Dry Puppy Dog Food.

4. Natural Balance Limited Ingredient Diet Dry Puppy Food.

For wet food, I recommend checking out these options:

1. Blue Buffalo Wilderness High Protein Grain Free – Natural Puppy Wet Dog Food.

2. Canidae Pure Grain Free Limited Ingredient, Premium Wet Dog Food.

3. Purina ONE SmartBlend Natural Puppy Dog Food.

Please always read up to date reviews before you choose a food.

By the time you read this book, these recommendations may change, but as of now, early 2020, these options would be the best place to start for your husky pup.

I've also heard a lot of great reviews about the two brands ORIJEN and INNOVA. But I am yet to try them. I would check out their puppy food options as well.

Ideal nutritional breakdown of a husky puppy's diet

Siberian huskies, young and old, thrive off of protein and fat. You'll need to make sure the food you are giving your husky puppy contains a minimum of 20-22% high-quality protein from whole meat, and 8-10% of healthy fat. This information will be displayed on the packaging of your puppy's food.

This short breakdown covers the important macronutrients in any husky's diet.

- **Protein**. Protein should come from whole meat sources such as chicken, beef, fish, and lamb. Sources like duck, salmon, and turkey are even better as they are not common allergens.

- **Fat**. Adequate fat should come from healthy sources like flaxseed.

- **Omega 3 and 6, DHA**. Omega 3 and 6 fatty acids are essential for healthy brain function, eye and retinal development, immune system support, and, help maintain healthy skin and coat. DHA is one of the Omega 3 fatty acids and is commonly found in the mother's milk.

- **Carbs**. It's important to keep your husky's blood sugar level constant. Ensuring carbs are low will help with this. On top of that, it's good to choose a dog food that uses a low glycemic carb like sweet potato that digests slowly.

- **Calorie Density**. Siberian Huskies are notoriously fussy eaters and will happily skip a meal. Making sure their food is high in calories and nutrients will ensure they are getting the adequate nourishment they need.

- **Calcium to Phosphorus Ratio**. Puppy foods should contain a calcium to phosphorus ratio of 1.2 parts of calcium to 1 part of phosphorus. An imbalance of this can lead to problematic health issues. This information should be located on packaging of your puppy's food. If it isn't, I recommend checking the company's website for this specific information.

- **Avoid Irritants**. It's best to **avoid foods that contain** common digestive irritants like wheat, corn, soy, as well as fillers, by-products or artificial preservatives, flavors or colors.

- **Avoid Lactose**. Most Huskies (or any dog breed) are lactose intolerant. So it's best to avoid food containing milk, whey or powdered milk ingredients.

Food items that should be avoided

There's quite a lot of food that dogs and puppies should not consume. Some of them you may not be aware of!

Here's the list of food ingredients and items that should be avoided:

- Chocolate
- Coffee (caffeine in general)
- Salt
- Alcohol
- Mushrooms
- Onion, Garlic and, Chives
- Cooked Bones
- Xylitol (found in candy, chewing gum)
- Sugary Items
- Yeast
- Macadamia Nuts
- Walnuts
- Raw eggs
- Avocado
- Cherries
- Citrus Fruits
- Raisins, Grapes, and Currants
- Figs
- Grapefruit
- Any pits from fruits such as plums or peaches

Some of these items are more common than others but all are toxic and some even cause choking hazards like the large pits in certain fruits.

What to do if your husky pup doesn't eat his food

This will likely happen at some point, so it's good to be prepared. If your pup stops eating his food it's best to do some troubleshooting first. This will allow you to make the best decision according to what the problem actually is.

Here are 3 reasons why your husky pup may not be eating:

- He's already sick or has health issues
- No defined feeding times
- He's sensitive to the food you're using

The first and most important thing to think about is if your husky pup is ill or sick. If he's vomiting, has diarrhea or you notice him acting unusual, it's time to visit your local vet for further checks.

It may not be sickness causing him to avoid his food if he's still happy, playful and bouncing around. It may be because he isn't hungry or his body isn't used to the times you're trying to feed him. Puppies are extremely adaptive so he will learn to eat at set times, this means he'll only be hungry at those times. Make sure you aren't trying to feed your pup at different times each day.

Lastly, the food you're using may be upsetting his sensitive stomach. You will probably notice his stools being somewhat runny or he may even have diarrhea. It can be tricky to know when his diet isn't working and some symptoms don't always show immediately. If your puppy isn't obviously sick, and you've been feeding him at consistent times, it may be time to try a different brand.

3 different solutions:

1. Double-check the food label. You should double-check the food label on your puppy's food or treats. It may actually contain some of the toxic items or common allergens that can upset your puppy's stomach. The use of dairy is still relatively high and this can cause issues for a lot of puppies.

2. Change the protein source to fish, duck, turkey, or salmon. For many people, the go to protein source is chicken, beef or pork. Those three meats are so common and are used in practically everything that it's normal to not think twice about them. But the truth is that they're all common allergens and can easily upset your puppy's stomach. Protein that comes from duck, turkey or salmon digests better and doesn't cause reactions. Try switching his protein source and monitor your puppy's reaction.

3. Add in extra flavor to his food. There are many healthy ways you can increase the flavor of your pup's food. You can include a small amount of natural meaty broth from your own dinner on top of his food. You could increase the amount of wet food he has mixed into his dry kibble. Or, you could add a small amount of organic salt-free peanut butter in with his kibble. These tips should make each meal time more appealing.

When to visit your veterinarian

If your pup doesn't eat anything for 2 days, you must visit your local veterinarian for extra help and tests. There's only so much that you can try and it's important for your puppy to get nutrients into his system.

Diet - key points

Here's a quick summary of all the important points covered throughout this section:

- Feed your pup the same food your breeder uses for at least 2 weeks after you bring him home.

- Transition your pup into a commercial food diet made up of 80% dry kibble and 20% wet food. Make the change gradually, introducing the new food slowly, and phasing out the old food over the course of 1-2 weeks.

- Ensure you use a dog food that is made for PUPPIES and ideally, choose a limited ingredient, sensitive stomach option.

- Feed your pup 3 times per day. Once when you wake up, again between 12-3pm and in the evening no later than 6pm. (or stick to the times your breeder used)

- Follow the portion size recommendation given to you by your veterinarian or breeder. You can use the packaging but like I mentioned above it's quite hard to know the correct portion size until you schedule a health assessment for your pup.

- If in the case your puppy is refusing to eat, make sure you visit your veterinarian if you haven't resolved the situation in 2 days. Your pup will need some further help and tests to find out what's wrong.

Before ending the section on diet, I would just like to point out that it's ok to visit the vet if you are unsure of anything. It can be hard to figure everything out on your own and puppies can be confusing. Your pup hasn't really worked out the best way of communicating, and you haven't worked out how to understand him yet, it's all-natural. If you're having trouble with his diet for more than 2 days, I would visit your local veterinarian as soon as possible to get the situation resolved.

Huskies From Around the World

This is Odin. He and his big beautiful blue eyes are 4 years old.
He's living his best life in Southern California, USA

MEET *Odin*
4 YEARS, FROM
CALIFORNIA, USA!

Teething

Just like with babies, puppies will lose their "baby" teeth or otherwise known as deciduous teeth to make way for a set of 42 beautiful adult teeth.

You may have heard from other dog owners that this time is "terrible" and you often find blog articles titled "SURVIVING" puppy teething. It is admittedly uncomfortable for your puppy, but perhaps not quite life or death!

It won't be easy of course, but there are ways and methods of helping your puppy through this challenging time. I'll first cover more of the basics of teething and important information to know, and then I'll get into how you can help your puppy when he starts teething.

What is teething and when does it happen?

The entire process involves your puppy losing his baby teeth all the way until he has his full set of adult teeth. For all puppies, this process is different. Some will find it more uncomfortable than others, and for some, it may last longer than others. Although one thing that never changes would be the discomfort it will cause your pup.

The discomfort that your pup will feel during this process will make him want to chew and bite everything. Chewing and biting will help to soothe his gums, increase blood flow and provide all-round relief. So in other words, teething means A LOT of chewing.

Your puppy will gain a set of 28 baby teeth around 6-8 weeks after being born... **The teething process begins!**

Husky puppy teething timeline:

This is a rough guideline that fits most, but not all. Teething can be an on/off process so keep in mind that some days your puppy won't display any signs of teething or discomfort and he may not be chewing as much. Then on other days, it's very noticeable.

- **1-2 Months.** The set of 28 baby teeth typically come in from 1 to 2 months of age.

- **3 Months.** The first sets of baby teeth to come out are the Incisors at around 3 months of age to make room for new teeth.

- **4 Months.** Your pup will continue to lose his baby teeth. While this is happening, the adult premolars and canines will start to show at around 4 months of age.

- **6-7 Months.** Finally, the adult molars start to come through at around 6-7 months. The rest of the teething will still be developing.

- **7-8 Months.** The full set of 42 adult teeth should be developed by 8 months.

Like I mentioned above, the process can be shorter or longer and all puppies are different. What remains constant is the discomfort he will experience, so let's move on to how you can help!

8 Tips for helping your teething husky pup.

The teething process can be long and grueling for your husky puppy. Imagine having a mixture of tooth ache with stinging gums for about 8 months, I don't think I could make it! I'm going to show you a few different ways you can reduce your puppy's discomfort AND one amazing bonus of this is that he'll be less inclined to chew and bite things he isn't supposed to. *Like your sofa and shoes!*

1. Cycle through toys to keep them high value

Having plenty of chew toys is a must but many owners make the mistake of leaving them down at all times. You may assume that your puppy, with his vast selection of toys, would never think twice about chewing on the chair leg… Oh no, my friend.

It's understandable to think having constant access to all of his toys, will ensure he doesn't start chewing anything else. It does make sense, but what you'll find is that your pup starts to get bored with of all his toys. If he has access to them there's no challenge anymore and his toys would no longer be appealing as when you first put them down. He'll start to get curious of that tasty wooden chair leg again.

It's recommended to cycle through different toys only leaving them down for certain periods of time. This way, you're not only giving your puppy something to chew on at all times, but you're also going to keep his focus and engagement on that item. Your puppy will think he's receiving a NEW toy, multiple times per day. That is far more exciting than your chair leg. Just remember to swap it out before he gets bored of it.

2. Rub peanut butter on toys

The goal of this is similar to the first tip, although it can be more powerful. Of course, a toy with super tasty peanut butter on it will without a doubt have your puppy's full attention.

But it's even better than that, you can create a good habit that *lasts*. Often times your pup will start out by sniffing, licking, chewing and biting the peanut butter covered toy and without even realizing he'll continue to chew that toy long after the peanut butter is gone.

Eventually, your puppy will like chewing on that toy simply because he's already done it so much. After a few days of putting peanut butter on the same toy, that toy will become his go-to chew toy, with or without the peanut butter. *It really works!*

Not only will you save your sofa, furniture, and shoes, but his constant chewing will give him the relief he's looking for.

3. Frozen Hand Towel

A little unconventional but one of the best DIY chew toys for a teething puppy. Take a small hand towel and drench it in water (or some weak chicken stock) then place it in your freezer. Check on it every hour and take it out before it's completely rock solid, that wouldn't be any use! Allow it to freeze but ensure it's still pliable, then offer it to your pup.

The coldness will soothe his inflamed gums, and the chewy texture of the towel will provide ultimate stimulation and pain relief.

A big word of caution with this option is to make sure your puppy does not chew off small bits of the towel and swallow them. This could get stuck in the intestines and cause a serious problem. Only give him this toy if you are there to supervise him. This toy works best while your puppy is under 4 months of age as he won't be strong enough to rip through the towel.

4. Interactive Toys

Interactive toys or "puzzle toys" are also a great way to keep your pup focused on chewing what he's *actually* allowed to chew.

Interactive toys are often hollowed out, and contain a space for you to insert a few small treats. There's usually a small hole where the treats can fall out if your pup figures out the puzzle of the toy. Your pup will usually just have to roll the toy in a certain direction until the treats naturally fall out. There are many different styles of puzzles toys and they aren't just limited to spaces where treats fall out, you can get options where he'll have to press a button with his paw in order for a treat to pop out; or, even bark in a certain way, but I certainly don't recommend this one for many simple reasons I'm sure you can work out! *3am… woof woof

What I find with puzzle toys is that they're great for really keeping the attention of your pup for a solid 30-40 minutes, but after that they lose their appeal. To keep it interesting you can change the treats you put inside, or have multiple puzzle toys and keep them in rotation. Both ways would work just fine.

5. Ice Cube Treat

Another frozen option to try out. For this you will need an ice cube tray. It's really simple, all you have to do is place one of your pup's treats in each ice cube section, top it up with water and pop it in the freezer. My husky mix absolutely loves this game, but be prepared for your room to get a little bit wet. If your pup is anything like my mix, he'll fling it around the room until there's no more ice! He'll have a great time, but it will be messy.

Even with a lot of flicking happening, your pup's gums will still benefit from the ice and it will provide some effective pain relief for him. One ice cube may not last very long so be sure to make plenty in one time. Although it's a great option, you'll need to pay close attention to the number of treats your pup consumes!

6. Rope Toys

When choosing a rope toy, I strongly recommend getting one that has a lot of 5 star reviews. Rope toys always range in their quality and some are shockingly bad. With huskies being heavy chewers, it's a wise move to invest in a good rope toy that's strong and durable, or you may just find yourself replacing it every couple of weeks!

There's a great rope toy bundle on the husky supply page on My Happy Husky. I recommend checking it out before you make a rope toy purchase.

7. Chew Treats

If your puppy needs an excuse to get a juicy chew treat, teething is a great one! Certain treats can be organic, natural and provide daily dental health if chewed on regularly. A really great option would be the natural beef chews from Nature Gnaws OR check out a brand called Whimzees who specialize in chewy treats.

Although giving treats is a recommended way to help your pup through the teething stage, you have to consider his caloric intake and how it affects his mealtimes. Your pup's real food is more nutritionally complete than treats so it's crucial he eats all of his meals. If you suspect that his consumption of treats is negatively impacting mealtimes, reel back a little and make his puppy food a priority.

8. Frozen Carrots

A true classic that sounds like it came from your grandma! For an inexpensive, healthy DIY chew treat. Take one large carrot and freeze it. Avoid using baby carrots as they can pose as choking hazards.

This is a tried and tested method and despite sounding a little boring, actually proves to be quite a hit with nearly all puppies. If your puppy doesn't get along with chew treats or you just prefer the idea of giving him real food, frozen carrots will be a very healthy alternative. As well as benefiting from many vitamins and minerals, your pup's teeth will enjoy a thorough cleaning session. As you can see, there are many great benefits to the frozen carrot idea.

Before rushing to the supermarket to buy all of their carrots; it's recommended that you only give your pup one large carrot per day. Due to the high fiber content, too many carrots could upset his stomach and digestive system.

Looking after your pup's teeth

In the beginning, before your pup has all of his adult teeth, most cleaning will be taken care of through his unlimited chewing on various textures. Chew toys, with all of their little nooks and bumps will do a great job of removing plaque and keeping his teeth clean.

However, as your pup gets around 8 months old, towards the end of the teething process, it's a good idea to start taking matters into your own hands.

Oral health is extremely important for all dogs, and it pays to know how to look after your husky's teeth.

Start a brushing routine

A best and easiest way for you to start cleaning your puppy's mouth and teeth is with your finger. In these early stages, your finger can rub and clean your puppy's teeth better than you think. Just be careful! His teeth are going to be extremely sharp.

It's advised only to do this late in the evening while your puppy is calm and ideally already half asleep. Cuddle up to him and gently stroke his face, head and nose area, after he's aware of your contact, go in his mouth with your index finger and gently rub around the teeth and gums, without disturbing him too much. Keep the pressure light and remember this isn't something you've done before so it will be unfamiliar for him. That's why it's important to do it whilst he's in a very calm, sleepy state.

After many times of doing this, your puppy will be used to this new routine and you can swap your finger for a rubber puppy toothbrush and dog toothpaste. One thing that I've always found so amusing is that you can get beef flavored toothpaste. Try opting for a dog toothpaste that avoids using nasty chemicals. If you're able to find a natural ingredient version, I would go with that to be safe.

Be sure to inspect his teeth frequently and try cleaning them 2-3 times per week. If you feel like they need more or less cleaning, adjust your routine accordingly.

Schedule check-ups

On top of doing your best to clean his teeth yourself, it's also wise to have some dental check-ups with your local veterinarian for a thorough inspection.

A veterinarian will be able to perform proper tests and they have the expertise to know when everything is fine, and when it's not. It may be an extra cost for you but considering that dental health can be life-threatening, it's worth it. Twice a year is all your husky needs and then you don't have to worry.

Over 80% of dogs show signs of gum disease before they're three years old. This is an alarming number and shows the significance of oral hygiene. Try your best not to neglect it!

Chew toys

It must seem like chew toys are the key to everything by now! Well, not everything, but they are good for keeping your husky's gums and teeth healthy.

Chew toys can help the gums by stimulating them and providing great blood flow. For the teeth, they can help remove plaque and tartar build-up which can lead to further oral hygiene issues.

Always be careful with the type of chew toy you opt for. Huskies, in particular, are aggressive chewers that can shred a lot of toys. Be sure that the toy is not going to break and cause a choking hazard. This will be more of a concern to you as your puppy reaches 6 months of age, at which point he'll be more than capable of ripping most toys you give to him. For now, just remember to always supervise your puppy with toys and never leave toys down that could be choking hazards.

Teething - key points

Here's a quick summary of all the important points covered throughout this section:

- Teething starts around 1-2 months when he gains his set of 28 baby teeth.

- At around 3 months your pup will start to lose his baby teeth over the course of several months to make way for his adult teeth.

- In most cases, your pup should have his full set of 42 adult teeth by 7 or 8 months old.

- Teething is not a constant process, some days it will irritate your pup more, and on other days it may not be noticeable.

- Teething can be very painful and uncomfortable for your puppy. This usually changes his chewing and biting habits, and even his temperament.

- Have plenty of ideal chew toys that will stimulate his gums.

- Don't leave ALL toys on the floor, only keep 1 or 2 down and keep them in rotation. This will ensure your puppy doesn't get bored of having the same toys all the time.

- Use peanut butter to have your pup chew on a single toy for hours. Do this every day and you'll form a strong habit of chewing on that specific toy, eventually, you won't need to use peanut butter.

- Freeze toys, and make your own DIY frozen treats. The cold will help soothe inflamed gums and will provide a lot of pain relief.

- Ensure you start cleaning your puppy's teeth once the teething process has finished and he has his full set of adult teeth.

- Schedule dental check-ups twice per year to ensure his oral hygiene is in check.

Huskies From Around the World

This is Aspen. This cutie pie is from the United States!
She's 19 weeks old.

Grooming Your Puppy:
All You Need to Know

It's now time to go through the wonders of grooming. I'll cover everything you need to know from brushing and brushes, bathing and shampoos, dealing with shedding, as well as general grooming tips to keep your pup's skin and coat healthy.

Before I get into the main advice and grooming tips, it's important to talk about his coat. Your husky's luscious coat isn't just for looks, although it will certainly turn some heads, it's actually very important for his overall health. Each layer has specific roles in keeping your husky healthy and safe throughout his entire life. The topcoat is made up of long coarse hairs that provide protection against the suns UV rays and direct heat. It also acts a barrier stopping unwanted dirt and insects from reaching the skin. Then we have the undercoat, which is incredibly soft and fluffy providing valuable insulation in cold weather. It's also the layer that sheds upon seasonal changes, typically being twice a year, but this varies and depends on the countries climate you live in. If you live in a particularly cold country, you'll find that your husky sheds less, and he may even experience just a single coat "blow" per year, instead of the usual two.

It's now easy to realize just how valuable his two coats are. They play a significant role in regulating his body temperature, not just in cold weather but in warm weather too. This brings me on to quite a hot topic. **Shaving and cutting**. It surprises me that I still see this question asked but to some extent I can see why. "Can I shave my husky" is searched on Google thousands upon thousands of times, every month. The only answer is NO; unless he needs to be shaved for medical reasons or surgery. Without his coat, your husky has no defense to the outside elements. He'll no longer be able to regulate his body temperature, even in "normal" conditions. What's worse is that once his coat is shaved it may never grow back properly again. Some unfortunate huskies have been shaved and they didn't grow their coat back. Other huskies had their coat grow back, but only to form a matted mess that's irreparable. As the undercoat grows much faster than the topcoat, they often bind together while growing back, creating a sticking Velcro like texture. This also makes it virtually impossible to regulate body temperature. One reason people think to shave their husky is to help them cool down, which now you know would actually only help them to overheat! The other is to avoid shedding which may work, but when it means sacrificing your husky's health and safety, it's still a no brainer.

After clearing that up, let's move on to bathing and shampooing!

Bathing and Shampooing

Grooming is a term that covers a lot, so while brushing will be something you regularly partake in with your husky, bathing won't be. Siberian huskies are a very hygienic breed. It's quite rare to come across a husky who smells or has that typical doggy odor. Of course, if your puppy goes and rolls in some muck or foul substance, you'll have to go ahead and wash him. Aside from this, bathing will not be as regular as you may have thought.

When should you give your husky his first bath?

A general safety guideline given by veterinarians is that you should not bathe your puppy until 1-2 weeks after his second set of vaccinations; by which time he'll be around 16-18 weeks old. While being vaccinated, a puppy's immune system and general body function are weakened significantly. The shock of being wet mixed with his inability to regulate body temperature, makes bathing quite risky in his early weeks. Hypothermia poses a big risk to young puppies and it must be avoided.

What to do if your puppy gets dirty before 16 weeks old?

If your pup rolls in something foul, you can **spot clean** him to remove the substance. Physically remove as much of the muck as you can just by using your hand *(use a glove too!)*, then use a small damped rag or towel with puppy shampoo and clean locally, making sure the wet area stays as small as possible. Dry thoroughly, and then continue to use a brush to remove the rest, if any.

How often should you bathe your pup?

After you give your pup his first bath, he won't need another one for a good 2-4 months (providing he doesn't roll in anything). The best frequency to bath your husky is around once every 3 months. Although you may enjoy giving your pup some soapy baths, it's not good to overdo it. Here are some reasons why you need to avoid over-bathing:

Why so infrequent?

- Siberian huskies do a lot of self-cleaning, similar to cats.
- Huskies do not have naturally greasy or oily coats.
- Too many baths risk drying out your pup's fragile skin.
- Too many baths can actually increase oil production and make his coat dirtier which is completely counter-productive.
- Husky pups are very susceptible to hypothermia when wet.

Tips for when you do eventually bath your pup

- Your pup can't regulate his own temperature very well so be sure to use water that is body temperature, around 37 degrees. Contrary to popular belief, you should not use warm water. This increases the chances of hypothermia when the bathing stops.
- Bathe your pup indoors, in a warm room.
- Take it slow and be very gentle with your pup while he's in the water. His experience now will affect how easy or hard it will be the next time around.
- Use a puppy-friendly, natural ingredient shampoo. Many shampoos contain harsh chemicals and can strip your pup's coat and skin of natural oils. I've recommended some options below.
- Baby shampoo is the only safe alternative to an all-natural puppy shampoo. Baby shampoo is incredibly mild and doesn't contain harsh chemicals, perfect for any puppy.

PLEASE do not use regular human shampoo as its far too strong.

- You must thoroughly dry your puppy after bathing. Use a towel to pat him down until virtually dry. You may use a hair dryer but ensure it's on the lowest setting; hair dryers can easily dry out your pup's skin. And remember to keep him indoors until he's completely dry.

Recommended shampoos:

Puppy-friendly shampoos that are made using only natural ingredients are what I recommend using for your puppy.

The issue with most of the mainstream shampoos is that they contain a lot of strong chemicals. It may make your pup smell like roses, but this isn't good for his coat or skin!

Opt for an all-natural, mild shampoo. If it's organic, that's even better! Check out some of these recommendations below. I like these ones and many other owners praise them too.

1. Pet Pleasant Natural Puppy Shampoo

2. Paws and Pals Natural Puppy Shampoo

3. Earthbath All Natural Pet Shampoo

Brushing and Brushes

A very important part of your husky's life is his brushing routine. His double-layered coat will need regular maintenance brushing which will only increase as shedding season approaches. You have all of this to look forward to but right now, your little pup doesn't require the same amount of brushing compared to an adult husky. After all, your pup doesn't even have his adult coat yet! His hair will still be relatively thin and his skin will be very fragile, so it's important to ease in slowly when you start your brushing routine.

Although your pup doesn't need a lot of brushing right now, it's still important you introduce him to it. The sensation of being brushed is something that puppies usually take a while to adjust to. Remember, anything that your puppy has not already encountered after 12 weeks will be treated with extra caution and it'll be harder for him to be comfortable with. I recommend starting a simple brushing routine from the moment you bring him home, this way, you won't go wrong.

Your pup will typically go through a complete shed of his puppy fuzz around 10-14 months old. He'll lose his wispy undercoat and it will make way for his double-layered "adult coat" After this, you'll need to follow a more standard brushing routine which I'll go through below.

Let's take a look at a brushing timeline you can follow.

2 months of age:

Most of you will bring your pup home when he's two months old, which is still another month before the 12 week window. It's a great idea to introduce your pup now to his brush while he's still at a very accepting age. Remember that it's not necessary to focus on brushing for the purpose of removing hair right now.

Introducing the brush for the first time:

Try sitting down with your pup on the sofa or your lap; with one hand, hold his toy out and in the other hand have your brush. Although he'll prefer his toy, he'll be well aware of the brush and will want to inspect, that's fine, let him, but always bring his attention back to his toy. **That's the first step, easy right!** Keep on this stage for a short while before touching him with the brush itself. While briefly making contact, ensure you have that exciting toy dangling out in front of him, ready to steer his attention away from the brush. It's important not to let him become too fixated on the brush, it may start to irritate him or even scare him, that's why it's really important to have a high-value toy present. That's all you really need to do for the introduction phase.

After your puppy has had plenty of time with the brush getting used to it and understanding what it's for. You can start a gentle brushing routine 2 or 3 times a week. I can't stress enough that it only needs to be a gentle brushing. Before your pup has his adult coat there's not a whole lot of shedding happening anyway.

Opt for a routine of 2 or 3 times per week, and it only needs to be about 15-20 minutes at a time. Keep the brushing incredibly light and remember it's only about going through the motions preparing him for adulthood.

The reason I recommend owners doing this from such a young age is to teach your pup to enjoy brushing. It can be a really pleasant experience for him and it's even quite therapeutic for us! The last thing you want is an adult husky that's terrified of being brushed. Instill good habits early and it will pay off in the long run.

Adult brushing routine

At around 10-14 months when your pup develops his adult coat, he'll start to shed, and this is when brushing becomes a lot more important. Thankfully, with all the time that he's had getting familiar with brushing, increasing the frequency won't be a problem.

The best advice I ever received in regards to managing husky shedding is "little and often". This is so true and will save you many headaches! A common mistake I see, is when owners *forget* to brush their husky and then try to make up for it with a 2 hour long brushing session, expecting to remove all of their hair. It just doesn't work like that, and after spending so long brushing you become frustrated as to why it didn't work! I've seen it happen many times, and it's not the way to go. If I could only give one piece of advice for managing your husky's coat, it would be "little and often". Brush your husky for short periods, frequently throughout the week. Aim for 3 or 4, 20 minute sessions per week and you'll find that this is far more effective than one 2 hour long session.

Choosing the right brush

There are many types of brushes on the market and it can be really confusing when you want to purchase one! Fortunately, when it comes down to it, your husky puppy will only need one type of brush in the early stages. Before his adult coat actually develops, there's really no need to get any of the *fancy super-duper* brushes on the market.

The best brush to start with for your puppy:

By far the best and safest brush for your pup will be a Pin & Bristle brush combination. As the name gives away, you get two different styles of brush; one side contains the strong metal pins, and the other has soft plastic bristles. I personally love this brush due to its simplicity and strong build. You would be surprised just how many brushes out there now contain various mechanical parts and while they add functionality, they tend to break often. I advise to stick to one of the classics.

The bristle side is made up of thin flexible plastic bristles, much like a toothbrush. These are very forgiving and gentle on your pup's coat and skin. Although this won't actually do much in terms of grooming, it's a soft and safe way to introduce the brush to your pup.

On the other side, you have the pins. These are metal pins with smooth plastic balls on the end. The balls are very comfortable and smooth on your puppy's skin. This side of the brush is more efficient in terms of grooming, but once again, at this early stage, you aren't going to try to remove hair.

Brushes for when your husky has his adult coat:

Once your husky has his adult coat, I recommend arming yourself with two brushes. With these two brushes you'll be able to do everything you need for a complete brushing session. The first brush will be a simple undercoat rake, and the second brush will be a slicker brush. I'll explain a little bit about both of these below.

An undercoat rake will remove the most amount of dead hair, in the least amount of strokes. They're simple, cheap, and oftentimes don't break like fancy de-shedding tools do. De-shedding tools typically have different layers and buttons to push out the collected dead hair. In my experience, brushes with these mechanical parts don't have a very long life. It's best to stick to a solid, simple undercoat rake.

The next brush would be a slicker brush. Another simple design, but with a slicker brush you have very thin wire pins that are also shallow in depth. This brush is designed to finish off your husky's top coat, and it will do a mighty fine job of it too. Again, these brushes are cheap and will last a long time.

Using these two brushes combined will provide a great all round grooming session for your husky.

General brushing tips for your husky

Here are some extra quick tips that should help you with your brushing routine, especially as your pup grows from puppyhood to adulthood!

1. Inspect your husky's coat frequently

They say prevention is better than cure, and that's certainly true! It's so much easier to prevent any would-be tangles or matting rather than trying to resolve a full-blown mess. The more you check and inspect your pup's coat, the more chance you'll have at spotting them at an early stage. Matting has no exact shape or look, anything that resembles his fur clumping together can be considered as matting.

2. Make grooming time enjoyable for your husky

Grooming time should be a pleasurable experience for your dog and for you, not a grueling task. It's very common to hear "my husky doesn't stay still!" Try to choose a better time to groom your husky, preferably after exercise, when he's tired. By doing this you are increasing your chances of him being more calm and receptive. If you can make it so he enjoys it, grooming will be a breeze.

3. Always brush in the same direction as his coat

A lot of people think that brushing against the direction of the coat will remove more dead hair, but in fact, this isn't true. Going against the coat will not enhance grooming; all it will do is cause discomfort and potentially tangle his coat.

4. Remember the purpose of the brush you're using

This may sound obvious but always remember what brush you are using and what purpose it serves. It's all too easy to forget that you're using a slicker brush and all of a sudden find yourself trying to de-shed your husky...that will not work! Likewise, don't use a rake if you're trying to remove debris from the topcoat.

5. It's always better to start off light

For some brushes with shorter teeth, it's very unlikely that you will cause any pain or discomfort to your husky. But with longer teeth, you need to be more careful with how much pressure you're applying, even if the teeth are rounded and smooth. Start your brushing routine off lightly, evaluate how much fur you're getting out and think about your pressure. It's better to have many short sessions that your husky enjoys rather than a long painful session trying to get every last hair out. Remember, never press down too hard!

6. Inspect your brush every time before using it.

This goes especially for Pin brushes. Pin brushes have metal wires with small plastic balls on the end to avoid scraping the skin. If the smooth ball comes off from any of the wires, this may cause scratches or even cut your husky's skin. Undercoat rakes also have long metal pins and if one were to chip or break, this would leave a very sharp edge. Always thoroughly inspect the brush before you use it. One bad experience may cause your husky to fear brushing in the future.

7. Create a regular brushing routine to avoid matting

If you do not have a solid grooming routine in place, your husky's coat can mat pretty quickly. This is super important when it comes to the winter months as matting on the topcoat can ruin the insulating properties of the undercoat. Remember to inspect frequently on top of brushing 3-4 times per week. Little and often should be running through your mind by now!

8. Start at the head and work your way down

Whenever you start brushing your husky, it's good practice to start from the head and work your way down throughout the body ending at the tail. It's easier to know where you've already brushed and it makes the entire process a lot more efficient.

9. Reward your husky!

Whenever you finish your brushing session, be sure to give your husky some praise and reward him with a tasty treat. Keep up the good association with brushing, and it will only make next time even easier.

I hope this section has you feeling more confident about the grooming process. I admittedly used to dislike grooming, but I realized that I was thinking about it in the wrong way. I was too worried about considering it to be a "task" when in fact it's better to think of it as a fun bonding exercise. Even now I still can't believe I'm writing that! But it's true, brushing or bathing doesn't have to be something to dread. If you introduce your pup slowly and in the right way, he will honestly love it! Getting the brush out of the draw will have him wagging his tale with excitement and when you call bath time, he's standing there in the tub waiting before you know what's what. When your husky enjoys the process this much, it will be hard for you not too as well.

Clipping your puppy's nails

It's that time! Clipping nails will be an important part of your overall grooming efforts and something you will have to do fairly regularly. Up until around 6 months of age, your puppy will be growing rapidly, and he'll need his nails cut about every 2 weeks. But, this *can* vary depending on his diet and individual growth and his nails may need trimming a little more often. When your puppy becomes an adult and receives more frequent exercise outside, it's likely that you will only need to cut his nails 5 or 6 times per year. This will also depend on the types of surfaces that he regularly walks on.

Before we get into it! If you are really uncomfortable clipping your pup's nails, you can always take him to a professional groomer and have them do it. I completely understand that this part of grooming is the least enjoyed! But, hopefully after this chapter you will feel more confident taking it on yourself.

I know what you're thinking, "my puppy is going to hate this!" but it doesn't need to be the case. I know that many dogs dislike having their nails clipped and this is usually due to a bad experience they have received beforehand. Fortunately, with your puppy, you can set a good standard and make the process no big deal.

When to clip your puppy's nails

It's actually very similar to us, so take a second to think about your own nails; when the ends of the nails start getting too long you can see the white section of the nail. This is similar to your husky too and will be the part that you cut off. Sometimes this can be a little more difficult to see on your pup, so here's a clever trick you can use to be sure.

Your pup may have light nails, or dark nails. The color becomes significant because it actually makes it much harder or easier to see where the excess growth is compared to the actual nail that you want to keep.

If you're unsure where the excess nail is, you can use your phone's flashlight and place it on the floor pointing upwards. You can hold your puppy's paw and nails over the light and with the light shining through you will clearly see where the excess nail is and where the "quick" of the nail starts. The quick of the nail is the part that you do not want to cut, this contains veins. If you cut too close to the quick it's possible for your pup's nails to bleed a little which of course we want to avoid! The flashlight technique will help you avoid doing this.

Introducing the clippers to your puppy

Before you go ahead and actually try clipping your pup's nails, I recommend introducing the clippers to him first. This way, he will already have some familiarization with the clippers which should stop him being overly worried or concerned about them for the next time he sees them. While you're sitting down giving him some love and playtime, add the clippers to the equation and put them on the floor in front of you. He'll likely inspect them, sniff them and check them out. This is fine, just keep distracting him with his toy and make no big deal out of the clippers. As you progress, occasionally pick them up and touch his paws with them; once again make no big deal and resume the fun and games with his toy. Do this 2 or 3 times before you go ahead and cut his nails. This will ensure he is familiar and comfortable with the clippers making contact with him, before he ever has his nails cut.

How to clip your puppy's nails

There are two ways to go about trimming your husky's nails. You can use clippers or you can grind them. Grinding seems to be an increasingly popular technique which many prefer over clipping. However, clipping is actually significantly easier while your husky is still a puppy. Grinding could be a good option for when your husky is older with tougher and bigger nails, but for now I would stick with clipping.

The actual process of clipping

1. The ideal starting position is where your puppy can remain somewhat still and be very comfortable. If it's possible I recommend having your puppy lay in your lap while you're sitting down on the floor. Before starting it's important he seems happy to stay in that position for at least a few minutes. You can offer him a toy to chew, or give him a belly rub. Whatever helps him to stay in one spot.

2. Set up the phone light or torch turned on, facing upwards on the floor in front of you.

3. It's important to understand that your puppy is NOT going to stay perfectly still. This almost never happens. So you will have to allow him to be fidgeting somewhat. As long as he's not physically trying to jump away or run away, you can begin.

4. With a firm grip you need to hold his ankle and paw over the light. Here you will see the end of the nail. You should see a clear difference between the excess whitish translucent end part of the nail, compared to the quick.

5. This end part is dead nail and is fine to nip off with the clippers. So with your firm grip, control his paw, go ahead and make the clip. Be confident and quick with it.

6. Remember, your pup will be fidgeting a little and this is ok! As long as you have firm grip and control of his paw and the location of his nail inside the clippers upon clipping. That is just fine.

The hardest part of the process: keeping him still.

The hardest part of the whole routine isn't anything to do with using the clippers or finding the correct point to cut. **It's getting your pup to stay still.** Let me run through some extra methods to keep your puppy still or at least distracted while you cut his nails

The most important tip I can give is to handle your puppy's body, legs, paws, face and mouth as frequently as you can many times each day. A puppy that is used to a lot of handling will almost always be better when you need to keep him still. This won't just benefit you with clipping nails; this will cover a lot of important activities from inspecting his mouth, cleaning his teeth, and brushing his coat. Get him used to your touch and the sensation of having his whole body handled. I guarantee you this will help. It's also important to handle his ears too, but you have to be careful and always remember to touch lightly, cartilage can be fragile.

Here are some extra tips to keep your puppy in the same place:

1. Give him a high value chew treat. Preferably some kind of bone or anything with flavor that will really distract him and keep him content laying still.
2. **Smear some peanut butter on a plate and put it next to him**. It will take your pup a good 5 or 10 minutes to lick off the peanut butter and this will send him into another world. You could clip his nails 20 times over by doing this. This works really well.
3. Clip his nails towards the end of the day after he has had most of his daily exercise. Anytime your pup still has a lot of energy would be a difficult time to keep him still.
4. You can try clipping his nails when he's half asleep, or even during his sleep. This isn't a preferred method but if you're having trouble with the tips above, I would try this next.

Cleaning your puppy's ears

Siberian huskies have big beautiful triangle-shaped ears, and by nature are very open to outside elements. This confuses a lot of people and some say this increases the amount of dirt that gets inside. This makes sense, because the ear is physically exposed and debris can easily get inside. Others say that because the ear is open, it actually allows for better air circulation and therefore keeps the ears cleaner.

It's true that the ears are not enclosed and do not flop down on top of themselves. This does allow for extra dirt and debris to get inside, especially when your husky decides to roll in the mud or run through the bushes. However, at the same time, it's equally as easy for the debris to come back out of the ears, due to them being so open.

So my advice isn't to get too caught up in this, and just inspect his ears once every 1 or 2 weeks. In general, huskies do not have dirty ears, but this doesn't mean there won't be times you need to clean them.

How to clean your puppy's ears

Cleaning your pup's ears **should not** involve flushing with water. If large amounts of water get inside the ear, it could quickly develop into an ear infection which will require a trip to your vet and medication.

While there are many different ear cleaning solutions out there, a favorite method preferred by a lot of husky owners is a simple DIY option. This has also been recommended to me before by various veterinarians, so it's fairly well-known.

1. Mix equal parts vinegar with water.
2. Use a cotton ball to dap in the solution
3. Squeeze excess solution out of the cotton ball
4. Gently open the ear with one hand
5. Use the other hand to wipe out and clean the inside of the ear with the cotton ball

6. Use a secondary cotton ball without solution to dry the inside surfaces.

Remember that you don't want a lot of liquid or solution to go in the ear itself. Making the cotton ball wet with the solution is all you need. The slight acidity in the vinegar will help to clean the surfaces and also prevents yeast build up. Yeast and many other forms of bacteria will not survive in an environment that's slightly acidic. Of course this will not last a long time, but it will certainly decrease the chances of bacteria building up.

Cleaning your pup's ears shouldn't be a big problem, and try not to worry about it too much. Whenever you make trips to the vets, you can always ask the vet to quickly take a look inside his ears to see how they're doing. A quick look from the vet will not cost you any extra, and you'll have a good idea of the condition of his ears.

Huskies From Around the World

Odin from California, it's time meet **Odin from Texas!**
Here, Odin Saleen is 1 year and 6 months old and from Bastrop,
Texas, USA

Training Your Husky Puppy
Everything You Need to Know

Training your Siberian husky correctly from puppyhood is *crucial* if you want a well-behaved, obedient husky throughout life. Although Siberian huskies are considered of average working intelligence, ranking 77th out of 138 other breeds, I feel they're much savvier than they let on. However, what comes with this "hidden" intelligence is some *not-so-hidden* stubbornness and mischievousness.

Before I go any further it's important I address a common opinion about how hard huskies are to train. Many people say that huskies are "too much dog for a beginner" this is a very bold statement and is not often said about many other breeds, so is it true? While I personally agree that huskies are "a lot of dog" I don't think they're "too much dog". If the owner is prepared and ready to give their time, focus and commitment to their husky and training routines, then there's no need to worry any further. Huskies are only "too much dog" for those who assume it will be easy or get a husky with the wrong mindset. As you're reading this right now, I have no doubt that you will be a fantastic owner who breezes through training.

Before I get into the actual training methods, it's absolutely necessary to cover some basic training philosophy. **This is so significant that it will either make or break your training efforts.** So let's get into it!

Training Philosophy

One of the most important parts of training is not what routine you follow, different trick you try or treat you use. It's *how* you train. The *way* in which you train your husky will be the deciding factor to your success. There are many different styles and approaches to dog training but through my experience, **Positive Reinforcement-Based Training is by far the No.1 style** for the quickest results and most pleasant training experience.

Positive Reinforcement Style Training is when you only praise and reward him for the behavior and actions he gets correct. When he makes a mistake you do not punish him, but simply guide him in the correct direction next time. The thing I love most about this way of training is that it's fun, happy and full of positive energy. There are no bad or negative moments for either you or your husky if you approach training in this way. I really believe it's a much healthier way to train your husky and it will build a better relationship between you and him.

To top it off, this style of training is actually the most efficient. You'll see much quicker results using positive reinforcement compared to other more strict training methods involving reprimanding. What's better than this... not only do you see quicker results, but you're building a better, and more trusting relationship between you and your husky. There's nothing more saddening than seeing someone shout a command only to see their dog cower and fearfully assume position. In cases like this, their obedience is based upon fear. This is something I know you do not want!

Why does this work best?

Many breeds, including huskies learn the best through association and repetition. If you add in some praise and treats along the way; It becomes positive reinforcement based AND a whole lot more powerful. When your pup gets a part of any routine correct, you reward him instantly. This builds association between the action he just carried out, with the command you used, and then being praised for it. The link building in your pup's brain has already begun and if you repeat that step just a few more times, praising each time he gets it correct. It's guaranteed to stick. Remember that this method involves no forcing; it's up to your puppy … If he want's praise and those tasty treats, he needs to sit after you say sit, and he'll remember this from the last time he did it. Believe me, this really works.

Rewarding your puppy often throughout training exercises will keep him excited for more training. A keen student is *always* the best student. It's in your puppy's best interest to listen to you throughout training, and once your puppy gets a taste of your praise (whether it be words or treats) he'll soon want more it.

The importance of breaking it down

Another crucial element to your training is how you break things down for your pup. This means making it easy for him; set him up for success and use any moment you can to positively reinforce throughout your training.

You're going to notice that throughout all the training methods I cover, I break the routine down into many small steps. This is really important and it's all about creating small wins for your pup. This keeps him interested, happy and eager to follow your commands. Imagine learning a new language and in the first class, your teacher spurts out an entire sentence, and expects you to immediately understand half of it… It has to be word by word, until we become familiar and remember what each word means, only then can we string a sentence together and understand it. The same approach needs to be taken when teaching your puppy anything. Break it down into very small steps, and reward him when he gets each baby step correct. As he becomes confident, progress further into the training. I will break down all the routines in the correct steps further below. Some will need breaking down more than others and you'll understand why when you put it in to practice.

Be ready for many mistakes and challenges – A word on reprimanding

Despite how well your husky pup will learn when you follow the advice above, there will still be mistakes made. Before he's shown something he'll have no idea what to do, and even then on after, it will take a series of successful runs, before your pup will learn to get things right. I'm not talking about whether or not your pup sits on command, or fetches his ball properly, as that's not too much of an issue to worry about right away. I'm referring to chewing items he should not be, messy potty mistakes all over your floors, things that may frustrate you!

It's so important to remain calm when your pup doesn't do as he's supposed to. Even if you've shown him where to poop, and what not to chew, it may still happen for a short while. Losing your cool and shouting or any other form of reprimanding will only work against you. Gradually making your pup fearful and worried is a one way ticket to behavioral issues down the line.

Punishing your pup for getting something wrong does not achieve anything of value. Your puppy won't really understand what's happening when he gets punished, all he will know is that YOU are the one causing the feelings of fear and anxiety that he's now experiencing. The main issue lies with the fact that your pup will not remember the reason why you're mad. The following day, when he's happily chewing away on your chair leg, he's completely oblivious to the fact that you shouted at him the previous day for chewing on your shoes. It just doesn't link up very well. So then you end up in a vicious cycle of reprimanding over and over again. And the only thing that's sticking is the negative emotions you're causing him to feel. So… that's why I don't suggest ever reprimanding or punishing your pup. Let's move on to what to train first.

What training to focus on first

Let's go through what training should come first.

There are two main areas to focus on first for training, that would be potty training and crate training. Your puppy is a non-stop poop machine, so without a shadow of a doubt, you need to implement potty training right from the moment you get home, *literally*! The next most important training will be crate training, which you'll actually need to use from the very first day. As long as these two are covered first, the other training sessions can come as and when appropriate.

If you're wondering what this handbook will cover, here's the list:

- Potty training

- Crate training

- Basic command training (sit, stay, come, down, leave it)

- Bite inhibition training

- Leash training

Potty Training

Potty training, AKA *The messy training*. It's important to remember that you won't be able to save every poop or pee and your puppy will catch you out at least a few times. So it's better to be prepared and accepting of it, in advance.

However, you can still do a pretty good job of anticipating when he may need to go by following the method below and learning about his **key poop moments**. Let's get into the training.

Make a designated area for doing his business!

This is the basis and first step of the potty training method. Find a designated spot created ONLY for doing his business, **this should be outside in your yard!** If you do not have a yard and you live in an apartment, you'll need to make this space inside, although this isn't ideal and you're going to have far more potty mistakes moving forward.

5 Step potty training method:

1. **Make a designated poop zone.** Create a small section of your yard for his potty training. Consider this a sacrificial piece of land. You won't be using it for anything else, anymore. Pick a piece of land away from the main area of your yard or relaxation area and far away from vegetable patches, if you have any. Once you pick a spot, don't change it, this will just confuse your young pup.

2. **Take your pup only to that spot after KEY moments.** The key moments your puppy will usually need to use the toilet is immediately after **playing, eating, drinking, sleeping, napping, upon seeing you for the first time after you've gone out, and before bedtime.** You should take your pup

there every single time! If you're lucky enough to have a lot of free time, it's a good tactic to simply take your pup outside to the spot once every single hour.

3. **Be patient, and use your command.** Have a simple command ready like "potty-time". When you make one, stick with it and don't use any other words, this can really confuse your pup. After any key moment or every hour, take your pup to the spot and wait there for 5-10 minutes. Be patient, at first, your pup may not really know what to do, especially if he doesn't need to eliminate. Keep using your phrase, and do not engage in any other communication or playtime. Keep him in the spot, repeat your phrase several times and wait. (If he doesn't go I will cover that below) As it's important to keep him located in the area, I recommend getting a small puppy pen so he can't go elsewhere. It's likely he will resist wearing a harness or leash until you introduce it to him so in the beginning, a physical boundary will be better. More on leash training later.

4. **Praise heavily upon any successful run.** Whenever your pup eliminates in the potty spot, you must praise him heavily! Give him a small tasty treat and use your voice to really hit it home that he has done well.

5. **Immediately leave the designed area.** After 5-10 minutes or as soon as he eliminates, praise him and leave the area. This area is only for potty times; the longer he stays in this area without going to the potty the less he'll associate it with doing his business.

Key points about this training

- It's really important to keep him in the area, use a puppy pen or leash and harness if he's comfortable with it.
- Avoid all playing/talking and only use a single command while in the area.

- Always take your pup after playing, eating, drinking, napping, sleeping, before bedtime, and seeing you first the first time after you've been out of the house.
- After the first successful run, leave the first poop in the area until the next time. Don't worry!! It won't take long! But it will definitely help him understand what this area is for.
- If he doesn't eliminate when you take him there, **don't praise or reprimand.**

What if your puppy didn't use the toilet?

There may be times where you take your puppy out to his spot and he doesn't eliminate. Here's what you should do in these situations.

1. Pick him back up, and bring him inside the house again.
2. Once in the house, wait a few more minutes, do not engage with him.
3. After a few minutes, pick him up and take him back outside to repeat the full process.

Why should you do this?

Puppies have very short attention spans, he may get distracted the first time and it's normal for him to misunderstand what you want from him on the spot. By repeating the process a second time, you are giving him another chance to successfully do his business in the correct place. **This is super important and if he does go, consider it a huge win!**

After the first successful run, you can be assured the connection has been made and with only a few more successful repetitions, he'll know where he should be eliminating. With a little more time he will learn not only to wait until you take him but if he needs to go, he will let you know!

When your pup makes a mistake inside the house

When he makes a mistake inside your house, try to remain calm, regardless of how bad or messy the crime is. This is the best course of action is as follows:

In a firm voice, say "No" the use of the word no is extremely important, and yes your pup will get a sense of his wrong doing by your tone and any other time you have used the word "No" in the same way. That's all you need to do to let him know it's wrong, **no shouting, no smacking, no shutting him away in another room.**

After you say "No", calmly take him outside to his potty spot where he should have gone and stay there for a few minutes, repeating your "potty-time" phrase. Of course, he has literally just relieved himself on your floor so he won't need to go again, but this is to show him where he should have gone, and trust me, your pup will understand what's happening. Especially if this isn't the first time he has made this mistake.

Come back inside and go on with your day. Reprimanding only builds fear and anxiety, which will negatively impact your puppy's confidence, which in turn, keeps him making the same mistake over and over.

Last thoughts on potty training

Despite this being a great method, there will still be times he makes a few mistakes. Perhaps you bring him back inside and he poops right there on your floor. Yup, it is what it is and you just have to be ready for the next time.

Remember to use positive reinforcement and praise him heavily when he gets it right.

Crate Training

Your puppy's crate is going to be very important in the beginning, especially while he's young and not yet house trained. The crate has a bad rep and is often seen by people as somewhere that puppies hate to be. While this can certainly be the case, *it shouldn't be!* If you introduce the crate to your puppy like I'm going to show you how, he'll become to love it and consider it his den or safe zone. There's absolutely no reason why your pup should fear or dislike being in his crate, but it can easily happen if he's forced into before he's comfortable with it.

It won't be long before you realize just how valuable it is for your puppy to go in his crate without a fuss, and be confident that he likes it in there. Although you won't like doing it, you'll have to leave him alone at some point. We all have busy lives and no matter how much we love our pup, we still need to leave the house, work, and go about our daily routine. These are all times your pup will need to go back in his crate and you'll want to know that he's happy in there while you're gone.

Important note: Be absolutely sure to remove collars before putting your pup inside his crate. This will avoid the chance of his collar getting caught and causing serious harm.

Choosing the correct crate for your husky

Getting the correct type of crate is important and will have a big effect on how successful your crate training is. Your pup needs to feel comfortable and safe in his crate, and the goal should be to make his crate very own den or safe-zone. While there are many tricks and ways to accessorize his crate in order for him to like it; nothing beats picking the correct crate in the first place.

There are a few different types of crates on the market; there are wooden crates which are also called "fashion" crates. These tend to be the option to go for if it *must* fit in with your home furnishings. Honestly, they look fantastic, but they're made from wood and while this is ok for some breeds, your husky is a BIG chewer, and having a crate made from wood is asking for bad habits. So, personally, I would avoid a fashion crate while he's young. This may be a great option when he's an adult and no longer chews what he isn't supposed to, but for now, keep it in mind. Another type of dog crate is the heavy-duty crate. As the name implies they're not be messed around with! These crates are typically made from thick, reinforced steel that's welded together. Initially, I can understand the lure of these crates, they're very well-made, your husky definitely can't chew or escape, and they're just an all-round quality crate. But, honestly, I think they're slightly *overkill* for a husky; unless your husky is half grizzly bear I'm not sure this crate would be necessary. This is an option better suited for larger, stronger dogs that have behavior or aggression issues. They're also extremely expensive, hovering around the $200 mark. So let's move on the crate I recommend.

What crate should you get?

I strongly suggest opting for a metal wire crate. This is the "normal" style of dog crate you may have in mind and is by far the most popular. But I'm not suggesting it because it's normal or popular. It's just the best all round option for a husky. Many of the wire crates come with two opening doors for increased ease of access. This feature actually makes the crate more inviting during the initial introduction stage of crate training; you can sit there with both doors wide open, which makes the crate feel less enclosed. Secondly, the doors typically come with a double latch system, which makes it virtually impossible for your husky to paw away at the door, until it opens. With Siberian huskies having such a natural talent for escaping, this is definitely something you have to look for when picking a wire crate. Another feature is having a pull out plastic cleaning tray, this is very helpful for when your pup makes potty mistakes; you can whip it out, hose it down, disinfect it and pop it back it. This typically isn't a feature for "fashion" crates. Metal wire crates are actually the lightest and easiest to move around out of all the different styles. This is of particular importance if you plan on only buying one crate, as in the beginning you'll need to have him sleep in his crate in your bedroom, then have it set up in his daytime area too. To top it off, wire crates are typically the cheapest type of crate out of the three.

Where should you put the crate?

As I mentioned above, it's necessary to have your crate in two different places; during the night it should be beside your bed and during the daytime it should be in his designated daily area. This either means moving one crate around, or investing in two crates. Fortunately, metal wire crates are not *too* expensive or heavy, so it's really down to you.

Putting your puppy in his crate at nighttime

When it comes to night time, your pup will be a little anxious, especially to begin with while he's still figuring out his new environment. One of the main reasons your pup will wake up during the night *(aside from potty breaks)* is sensing that his mother isn't beside him. This can really unsettle him and it's understandable too. By locating his crate right next to you throughout the night, it will give him some extra support, knowing that he's not alone. After you take your pup home, you become his new found guardian, the person to love him, care for him and make sure he's ok. It won't take long for him to know this, and he'll soon seek for your constant support. It's up to you how long you would like to have his crate in your bedroom, but I suggest allowing it until you know he's really comfortable with his crate and sleeping, regardless of his location in your house.

Where to have the crate during the daytime

During the daytime, like I covered in the **preparing your house** section it's important to make a designated daytime area. It's crucial that his crate is here throughout the day too, as it's where you'll be carrying out your crate training routines. It helps to make his crate in a room that's frequently used and fairly central to the house, the kitchen or dining room area is generally the preferred room, but it's entirely up to you. I do suggest using a room with hard floors, mainly due to potty accidents. But as your pup becomes house trained, you may move the crate elsewhere.

5 Step crate training method:

1. Set the crate up with both doors open and bring your puppy into the same room to let him inspect the crate at his own pace. At this very initial stage, do not urge him to go inside, allow him to sniff around and get familiar with the presence of the crate. It's even a good idea to start using the word "crate" whenever he gets near to or interacts with it. Do this for at least 15 or 20 minutes. Be sure to have an exciting toy with you, and constantly distract your pup away from the

crate before he gets too spooked. The goal here is to make him comfortable with the crate without him focusing too much on it.

2. After spending adequate time around the crate and allowing him to become familiar with it, you can start encouraging him to enter. A good way to get him inside is to throw his toy in there and let him retrieve it. But before he exits, grab the toy and initiate some friendly tug of war style play while he's still physically in the crate. It's really important that you spend a good amount of time on step 1. This ensures your puppy is no longer spooked by his crate, so being inside it with the doors open should not be too much of a big deal; especially as you're playing. Once your pup has experienced going inside his crate, try your best to keep him there, but without forcing him. Praise him while he's inside, give him a couple of small nibble treats, and be sure to have his favorite toy there. The ideal situation to have is your pup lying down in his crate chewing his toy without a care in the world. Really try to capture this moment and let him soak it in; allow him to spend a considerable amount of time like this before moving on the next step.

3. It's now time to start gradually closing the door, until you're able to shut it completely. But this must be done slowly and in small stages. If you go too quickly, it may spook your pup and undo all of your previous work. After **mastering** steps 1 and 2, encourage your pup to go inside once again and give him another high value toy he can focus on. It's best to wait until he's lying down, completely consumed by his exciting toy. While he's busy, without making a fuss or speaking to him, slowly close the door half way and leave it there. If he ignores you doing this, that's great and you can get ready to continue. If he doesn't like you doing this and he gets up and tries coming out, allow him to. It's still too early on to be forcing him in the crate and he can still become frightened of it. After he comes out, give him some time until you repeat the process. If your pup wasn't fazed by shutting the door

half way, go ahead and slowly close it completely but remain beside the crate afterwards. If your pup remains chewing his toy, you've done it! You have carefully and slowly introduced him to his crate without him seeing it as something to fear. Before you get too excited remember that you need to always allow him time to really get accustomed to it. If you try progressing too quickly, it may frighten him and undo all of your previous work. If at any moment he showed agitation when you closed the door, you'll have to take a step back and try again at another time before moving on to the next step.

4. Once your pup is able to stay in his crate with the door shut while you're beside it, the next step is for you to start moving away. Gradually create more distance between you and the crate, and if it feels right, you can get up and move around to the other side of the room. Gauge how your puppy is responding to this, if he doesn't care what you're doing or where you are, that's fantastic. If he gets flustered when you move away, you'll need to start from the beginning when the door is shut, and take it more slowly. Remember during these early stages if at any moment your pup wants to come out of the crate it's recommended you allow him to do so. This is just training and it's all about making him happy with his crate for when we actually need to put him inside and leave him.

5. After it's easy for your pup to be in his crate while you're in the same room. It's time to up the difficult by leaving the room for a short period of time. In the beginning I recommend that you only leave the room for 20 seconds or so. It sounds ridiculously short, but like I've said throughout, make it easy for your puppy by breaking it down into very small steps. Remember the training philosophy of taking it slow and setting your puppy up to win.

When your pup cries at night in his crate

I know how this goes… You've read all that you can in order to be prepared, just like you're doing right now with this handbook; but nothing can prepare you for being woken at 3am on a nightly basis by your pup. There's no information out there online that will make you feel better, in that exact moment! So, with that being said, I really hope you prepare for a few restless nights, at least in the beginning. Fortunately if you have a solid bedtime routine, his cries will not keep you up for very long. The following section will be your plan of action for when he starts crying during the night. There's a strong reference to the bedtime routine you should have in place, so if you missed that section, I recommend reading that first.

When your puppy cries at night, there can be three different reasons.

- Your puppy is not yet comfortable inside his crate
- Your puppy needs to use the potty
- Your puppy is seeking attention

Crate issues: legitimate

You may have been wondering by now, "how can I get my puppy comfortable with his crate slowly, if I need to put him in it from the very first night?" That's a great question so let's go through that. Well, there's a little difference for why you're carrying out the crate training above. Although that training WILL help your puppy at night, it's actually designed for the daytime, when you need to put your puppy in his crate and leave him while you're out of the house. For when you first bring your pup home, it's very normal for him to be extremely sleepy in the evenings. You have to use this to your advantage and after you've been through your bedtime routine allow him to become very sleep laying on your lap, then while he's half asleep put him in his crate for his bedtime. It's like getting a young child to sleep in their bed when all they want to do is stay downstairs, sometimes it's best to allow them to fall asleep, and then take them to their bed when they no longer resist. This will be your best course action until you've had adequate time running through the crate training throughout the day. Eventually your pup will be fine going to his crate to sleep.

Potty issues: legitimate

Your puppy may cry during the night for a legitimate reason, he needs to pee or poop! If this is the case, consider yourself lucky that he's even attempting to let you know, that's a great sign **which indicates your potty training efforts are working**.

I've covered exactly what to do in the sleeping section earlier on in the book. It's really important to have read this section on dealing with potty issues throughout the night first before moving on to the attention-seeking issues below.

Attention seeking issues: ILLEGITIMATE

Attention seeking is considered the *not-so-good* reason to be crying and it's important you deal with it in the correct way. If you respond directly to the *wrong* cries. You are confirming to your pup that's all he needs to do for you to come to him. Once he makes that connection it will be very difficult to deal with, and it will drive you insane!

So the biggest question here is, how do you know if your pup is just crying for attention? Well, this is why it's absolutely crucial to follow a good bedtime routine and establishing a time that you will take your pup to potty. Once you have these two things down and **you are positive that your puppy's needs have been completely met,** all further cries are simply for attention.

How to deal with cries when you think they're for attention? It's tough, but you need to ignore them. Responding to cries will very quickly solidify a bad habit, your pup will know that whenever he wants your attention, he just has to cry, and believe me, once he knows this, he'll cry a lot!

You have to be confident that your puppy's need have all been met; a great way to do this is to run through a mental checklist, before thinking about seeing to him.

Questions to think about:

1) Did your puppy have adequate potty breaks before going to bed?

2) Did your pup have his last meal 2-3 hours before bed?

2) Have you yet run through your mid-night potty break?

3) Did you expel his extra energy by playing with him before bed?

4) Does he have his snuggle toy or comforter?

5) Is his crate close to you?

Running through a checklist is a great way to work out if his cries are legitimate or just for attention. After running through the list you may realize he didn't go out one last time to relieve himself before bed. In this case, he'll likely be crying for a potty break. If you think it's for attention, grab your ear muffs and leave him be.

Basic Command Training

Having a solid understanding of the basic commands is considered to be the key of true obedience. Despite having to prioritize potty training and crate training before you implement basic commands, you should try to start these as soon as possible. Basic commands can often be overlooked. But in fact, they can enhance the communication and understandings between you and your puppy ten-fold. Could you imagine how easy everything would be if your puppy already knew what sit, stay, down, leave it and come here meant? You wouldn't be far behind getting him to cook the Sunday dinner! *Ok, back to reality.* In some ways, basic command training is actually the most important training for your pup to go through as these 5 skills will be used so much more than anything else you teach. Without realizing it, you'll be communicating with your husky almost entirely through commands involving sit, stay, down, leave it or come here. They are absolutely key. Fortunately, these commands aren't too difficult to start teaching. Let's get into it!

Let's take a look at how to teach each command with a few simple steps. Remember that your patience is necessary and you should always reward and praise when he gets it right, never punish him or show him your frustration if he's a slow learner. *Remember the training philosophy.*

Teach your husky puppy how to "Sit"

An easy and important command your puppy will be able to learn early on.

1. Start with a treat in your hand at let him know it's there

2. While facing your pup, hold your hand still, right in front of his nose

3. Once he's sniffing, slowly raise your hand up higher than him in front of his face

4. Use the command "SIT"

5. If your puppy does not sit, use your other hand to gently guide his backside down

6. As he sits down, repeat the command "SIT" again

7. Praise him and reward him with a treat. Repeat this process several times every day

Be sure to praise your puppy the moment he sits down. It's important for him to understand the link between him completing the action with praise and receiving a treat. Take it slow, and practice multiple times per day.

As your pup gets better at doing this, you can make it slightly more difficult by randomly instructing him to sit, without first getting his attention with a treat. With time, your puppy will master sitting down every single time. Practice makes perfect.

Teach your husky puppy how to "Stay"

The biggest benefit for your pup learning how to stay will be self-control. This goes a long way for overall obedience and will also help him to be calm in various situations. On top of that, knowing how to stay will significantly improve many other training exercises to follow. One other hidden benefit of stay that I don't often see anyone talking about, is how it will help stop your puppy from jumping up at people… Yep, it's a weird link but let me explain. By routinely carrying out "stay" exercises, especially when you're at an advanced level, it's building amazing amounts of patience and control. Ingraining patience and control in your puppy will change his overall temperament and you'll find that *any* dog, who knows how to be patient and calm, will not jump up. Although this has not been scientifically proven by the science gods out there, I've personally seen this correlation many times over. One to keep in mind!

As you normally always make your puppy sit before you ask him to stay, it's important that he's already got the hang of sit before moving on. Let's get into it!

1. While you are standing, command your puppy to sit

2. Use a stop hand gesture (open palm facing him)

3. Take one single step back while using your command "STAY" keep your hand raised with stop gesture firm.

4. If your puppy stays, go back to him and reward him with a treat and praise immediately

5. Keep repeating this but increase the distance that you are creating between you and your puppy each time.

6. Set him up for success and in the beginning do not make him stay for a long time.

7. Once he's mastered the steps above, start increasing the time you go without saying anything. The anticipation will build up and this will test your pup significantly. Remember to take it slowly and don't push him too far in the beginning. It's better to have many small wins gradually building him up.

Learning the "stay" command will almost definitely be harder to learn than "sit". The first time you try "stay", don't expect your puppy to understand, when you move, he's most likely going to follow you back.

Whenever he moves off the spot, calmly say "no", and walk him back to the original spot you made him sit. By doing this, He'll understand that he needs to try something again, especially as he isn't receiving any praise. Start in the sitting position and try again.

When you say your command of "stay", it usually works better if you say the word slowly. Vocalize the word as if you're dragging it out slowly, as you take a step back. This should help your pup remain focused on your voice, rather than the fact you have physically moved back. If you say "stay" very sharp and quick, this will excite your puppy and he's much more likely to run to you.

The moment you successfully step back and he remains in the same spot sitting down, go back to him and reward him with heavy praise and a treat.

Teach your husky puppy to "Come here"

Learning how to "come" is considered recall training; recall training is extremely important and is of particular importance when it comes to Siberian huskies. As you know by now, huskies just love being stubborn. It seems like their favorite command to defy, is "come here". I'm literally chuckling to myself while writing this. The moment you say "come here" to your husky, you've just entered into a dangerous game of pride and stubbornness. And let me tell you, he's already at the top level. He'll look back at you (if you're even that lucky) with a look on his face that you would never have thought possible coming from a dog. Don't worry you've got this all to look forward to! Anyway, let's get onto the basic training of "come here".

This training involves two people!

1. Both people will need to have a small handful of high value treats.

2. Each person should go to either side of the room and face each other, the closer the distance the easier the training will be for your pup.

3. One person should start by calling your puppy's name and saying "come here boy" It's really important to keep your tone happy, fun and energetic. It also helps to get eye contact and give him a big smile too.

4. It won't be long before your pup comes bounding over to you. In the moment he does you need to instantly praise him and give him one of the tiny nibbles, ensure you praise heavily.

5. While he's with one of you, the other person on the other side of the room does exactly the same, call his name and say "come here boy" in an energetic, happy way. Keep saying it until he comes bounding over to the other person.

6. When he does, reward and praise him heavily.

That's the basic version down! It seems too simple to work, but in actual fact it's one of the most tried and tested methods for learning "come here" It also has many follow up methods for making it more difficult.

After your pup can do this easily, you can change the game slightly to make it harder. This now involves only one person. Try using the same "come here boy" command when your puppy is least expecting it, again reward him if he complies. If your pup is responding to you most of the time at this stage, he's doing a fantastic job, and the more you carry out this simple training routine, the better he'll get at responding.

After you've mastered this exercise in your house, you can repeat ALL the above steps from no.1 outside in your yard where there are other distractions. This will be significantly harder, but you can use the distractions as an easy way to make the training tough.

Teach your husky puppy how to "Leave it"

This is such an important command that you'll soon realize you need to use very often. In case you've forgotten, huskies love putting everything in their mouth! It's also important for their safety; knowing to leave something alone can be a true life-saver. Your husky may unknowingly go to inspect a dangerous item like broken glass, spilt chemicals, or a toxic food. You may just avoid a trip to an emergency vet clinic if he understands "leave it"

1. You need two different treats, one should be more "boring" or less exciting, the other treat should be a high value treat like a tiny piece of turkey or flavored puppy treat.

2. Have the boring treat in one hand, and the exciting treat in the other hand. Place both hands behind your back and make fists.

3. Have your puppy sit down in front of you with his attention on you.

4. While you keep your fist closed, present the hand that contains the "boring" treat out in front of you. Keep the exciting treat behind your back.

5. When your hand is out in front of your, let your puppy sniff your fist.

6. When your puppy starts sniffing your fist, tell him to "leave it" and encourage him to back away. (as your puppy knows you have two treats, he will smell that this treat is not the high value one, so upon sniffing he'll be more inclined to step back)

7. As soon as your puppy steps back and stays there for a few seconds, praise him heavily and reward him with the high value treat that you've kept behind your back the whole time. When he steps back, if you could then command him to sit,

that's even better and you can consider that a further step to make it harder.

This training is simple but it works well for many reasons. Firstly, although one of the treats is "boring" it's still a treat, and it's quite significant for your puppy to resist something he can *actually* eat. Also, this particular training exercise gives your puppy a helping hand and encourages him to make the right decision. Your pup will know full well that you have two treats and his sense of smell is extremely powerful. He'll know that one treat is much tastier than the other, and when you present out the first fist with the boring treat, it's helping him to make the right decision of backing away, as hell be wondering where the other, more delicious treat is.

After your pup can successfully run through this training exercise without fail, he should have a good grasp of what leaving something alone actually means. You can test this out by using it in different situations. A great moment will be when you're playing with your pup and his toy. Like I mentioned earlier in the play section, try wiggling around his favorite toy, until he chases it and starts tugging back, make it clear you're playing by wiggling it around and moving it constantly. Then, bring the excitement to an abrupt stop, hold the toy dead still, make it boring as if you've stopped playing the game, and now in a more serious tone, use your "leave it" command. When your puppy lets go of the toy and backs away, give him some exciting praise and offer him a small treat. Keep practicing these routines, and he'll be a master of leaving things alone. This will prove particularly useful during his heavy chewing stage.

Teach your husky puppy how to "Lay Down"

This command, in theory, isn't hard for him to learn and the steps are very simple, but it will take some time before he will actually follow through with it by himself. Knowing how to "lay down" will prove to be extremely valuable for your husky when he's older, and out in public places. Huskies are very impatient dogs and often get jittery when they aren't on the move. But by having your husky lay down, it will automatically help calm him down and reduce his anxiety. "lay down" is like "stay" but on steroids!

1. Hold a treat in your hand.

2. Hold your hand in front of your puppy's nose so he can smell it.

3. Slowly lower your hand until it reaches the floor, and keep it there.

4. Let him follow your hand down and encourage him to "lay down".

5. With your other hand you may try tapping your finger on the ground next to your fist.

6. You may find that you need to use your free hand to **gently** apply some pressure on his backside.

7. Keep repeating the command "lay down".

8. When he is in the down/prone position reward and praise heavily.

9. Try to accomplish at least 3 or 4 successful repetitions of this in one go. As this is a little harder to grasp, I recommend doing this routine daily until he learns.

It may be better to leave this command to the end and focus more on sit, stay, come here, and leave it first. Those commands will be easier for your puppy to learn and will be more practical to know in his early months.

Like I mentioned above, basic command training should come as soon as possible, but this doesn't mean rush it. Take it slow, and focus on one at a time. Be very forgiving with your pup and know there will be a learning curve. It's better to go into the training expecting your puppy not to understand, than thinking it's going to be super easy for him. I recommend starting with "sit" within the first week two weeks of having him home. This is still very early for command training but in my experience, it has only ended positively.

Leash Training

The time will soon come when your puppy is ready for the outside world. Having him leash trained or at least comfortable with the leash is something you can do long before the big moment arrives.

It's a good idea to use a harness instead of a collar. A harness will avoid any unnecessary pressure around his fragile neck area. There will be many times throughout leash training that your puppy decides he doesn't want to go anywhere, so his reaction will be to back up. In these moments, if you were using a simple collar it could pop right off over his head. This isn't a good situation and it can even be dangerous if it were to happen in a busy public area. I really recommend opting for a simple harness for your pup. I have a good example on the husky puppy supplies page on My Happy Husky

The step by step leash training method:

The leash training process isn't very complicated, but it may take some time. The actual method is very easy, but it is broken down into a lot of small individual steps. I see many people quickly force the harness on, attach the leash and wonder why their pup is throwing a tantrum! The introduction process and familiarization steps are drawn out for a reason, to help your pup feel comfortable before moving forward.

Start by sitting on the floor with your puppy and have the harness and leash at the ready. You will need some small, high value treats for your pup and plenty of them!

1. Place the harness on the floor while entertaining your pup

- After putting the harness down, keep making a fuss of your pup, being sure to divert his attention away from the harness with a tasty treat.

- Let him sniff around but keep disengaging his focus. You don't want him to become too fixated on the harness as he may spook himself.

- By giving him some treats while the harness is on the floor next to him, it will start building positive associations.

- Keep on this stage until your pup really isn't bothered about the harness at all.

2. Making contact with the harness

- Let your puppy see you touch the harness and even move it around a little.

- Once again, divert your pup's attention away from it by offering another tiny nibble treat.

- Pick up the harness, touch your puppy's back with the harness and put it back down. Divert attention with further nibbles.

- The goal of this is to get your puppy comfortable making physical contact with the harness. It's a step up from just having it on the floor.

- At first he may give a negative reaction when it touches him and he may back away, run away, or even bite the harness. All of this is ok, put the harness back on the ground and break his attention again with your voice and some nibbles.

- Keep on this stage until he isn't fazed by physical contact with the harness.

3. Put the harness on your puppy

- After your puppy is fine with the harness touching him, actually go to put it on him.

- Keep using treats to divert his attention.

- Once it's on he may start to try and bite or chew it. This is okay; just calmly divert his attention before it becomes excessive.

- By now the style of this training should be clear. It's about taking baby steps and taking the time for him to feel comfortable on each stage. It's slow, but very effective.

4. Now place the leash on the floor

- Now it's time to introduce the leash.

- You guessed it; you should take the exact same approach with the leash as you did with the harness.

- Being attached by a leash can be a very weird sensation for a puppy, and if you just go ahead and clip it on without any familiarization first, it may easily freak him out. It's really necessary to keep the process slow.

5. Make contact with the leash

- After your pup is completely comfortable with the leash in his presence, go ahead try to start making physical contact.

- Tap the leash to the harness's hook to make a clipping sound. Allow your puppy to become familiar with the leash.

- Remember to go slowly, put the leash back on the ground, and divert his attention away. Once he's comfortable move on to the next step.

6. Attach the leash to the harness and drop it on the floor

- Once attached. Place it on the floor and your puppy will instantly know something has changed.

- Let him figure out that the leash is now attached to him. When he moves, the leash moves! This will be quite a weird sensation for your puppy and he may want to chase it or bite it.

- Give him some time and be ready with treats if he becomes too focused on the leash.

7. Pick up the leash

- Let your puppy know and see that you can hold the leash while it's attached to him.

- Walk back from your puppy and let him walk towards you.

- Divert his attention with treats and your voice.

Repeat this training on a daily basis and remember to go slowly, as you continue with the training, your pup will soon understand what the harness and leash are both for.

Tips for better training

Here are some helpful tips to ensure you're getting the most out of your training sessions.

- Use a comfortable harness that fits correctly, make sure it isn't too loose or too tight.

- Practice walking around your home on the leash, before going outside.

- Refrain from yanking or pulling your puppy. This will create negative associations with the leash and encourage him to pull back.

- Give your puppy praise and reward him when he's comfortable coming to you while on the leash.

- If your puppy is trying to pull you. Stand still and remain in the same spot. Let him get bored and reward him when he stops the pulling.

Whenever attempting to go through a leash training session, it's a good idea to pick a specific time of the day. One way to make it super hard for your puppy and yourself is training him when he is in need of something else. He won't be able to give you his full attention during the following moments.

Times to avoid starting a training session:

- If your puppy hasn't recently eaten and it's approaching the next mealtime

- If your puppy hasn't recently been for a potty break

- If your puppy has just woken up from a nap

- If your puppy has a lot of toys or people around him

- If your puppy hasn't received a good amount of exercise already for the day

Bite Inhibition Training & Chewing Control Techniques

Chewing and biting is something that all puppy owners have to go through. But, you didn't decide to get just *any* puppy... Oh no, you got a Siberian husky! That means you may have to deal with a little more biting and chewing than normal. Huskies are known to be very "mouthy breeds" and while most people consider this an issue, I don't think it's anything to worry about, as long as you approach it in the right way.

To begin with, your puppy does not know that biting your sofa or chewing your shoes is wrong, not until he has been told a good handful of times. So it's really important you keep your cool and never punish him in any situation that may happen.

Before we get into the training methods it's important to understand the main causes of chewing and biting.

Main causes for chewing and biting:

- **Your pup has started teething.** From as young as 2 months old, your pup will start teething. As I explained in the teething section above, the complete process can vary in length, but usually lasts several months. Throughout this time your pup will seek to chew and bite whatever he can, which will provide him some much needed pain relief.

- **Your pup is learning his bite threshold.** Your pup will explore the world through his mouth and he'll be constantly testing what he can bite, and how hard he should bite for whatever is inside his mouth. Believe it or not, this is a natural process and shouldn't be stopped. Knowing to chew differently on his kibble, compared to how he chews his rubber toy, all has to be learned.

- **Your pup is anxious or bored.** Where the previous two causes are healthy and to be expected, there's one other cause of chewing and biting that isn't so positive. If your pup becomes bored or anxious, it can lead to destructive chewing. If this were to be the case you would have to assess your puppy's daily routine, and ask yourself important questions like, has he been let out? Are you leaving him alone too long? Are you giving him enough attention? Does he receive enough training and mental stimulation? Has he received adequate exercise? In most cases, if your pup is bored or anxious, he'll develop a bad chewing habit regardless of knowing what's "right and wrong" Thankfully, these issues will not happen, if you're giving your puppy everything he needs.

One important point to make about his biting threshold; your pup needs to know when his bite hurts. As soon as your puppy starts nipping at your fingers you need to let out a loud "ouch!" before you think about handing him a toy instead. Your puppy needs to know this hurts. It proves to be an important lesson that will dictate how he plays with his mouth for the rest of his life. When puppies stay with their mother, their mother will teach them an unforgiving lesson when they nip and bite her tail one too many times.

The benefits of your puppy biting and chewing:

- The more your pup understands his biting threshold, the more he'll understand how to be gentle with his mouth too. This is a very important ability especially for when he meets young children and babies. Although it must be said, puppies are never really gentle; this skill comes with age.

- Chewing will provide effective pain relief when your pup is going through his teething stage.

- Biting and chewing will sufficiently develop his neck and jaw muscles. It will also ensure his ears rise up correctly.

- Frequent chewing on the correct style of toys can keep your husky's teeth clean and free from plaque build-up.

It's good to know the benefits of chewing and biting, but I know you're worried about your sofa, so let's get stuck in to the method.

How to stop your puppy biting and chewing thing he shouldn't be

This training method doesn't teach your pup to stop chewing or biting *altogether,* it focuses on showing him what he can chew, and what he cannot chew. This is an extremely important lesson to learn and if you don't show him at an early stage, he'll think he can chew anything he wants.

Stop and redirect your Husky's chewing in 4 simple steps:

1. Stop and Intervene

The moment your pup starts chewing something he's not allowed to, raise your voice louder than usual and in a firm tone say "STOP", you may include his name to be more direct. The point here is to **startle** him just enough to gain his attention for a brief moment. If this is a situation where your pup is biting your fingers, now you need to say "ouch!" abruptly, and then carry on with "stop"

2. Inform

The importance of understanding the word "NO" is huge! The best way to do this is through association. After gaining his attention with the command "stop", give him a firm "NO" in response to his chewing. Your negative tone will certainly be acknowledged and he will know that this is not acceptable behavior.

3. Replace

Now, after you've stopped and informed him, you must swiftly replace whatever he was chewing, with one of his favorite toys. Your puppy will not think he's getting a toy as a reward for chewing your finger as long as you carry out steps 1 and 2 correctly. Be firm with your "stop" and "no" and your pup will understand you're not happy. Giving him his toy will not be seen as a reward.

4. Praise

Once your puppy remains focused on his toy for a good 5-10 seconds, you can then give him good praise. Be sure you don't prematurely praise him, this will cause a lot of confusion and your puppy won't know if you're praising him for chewing your finger or the toy. He must completely focus on the toy you've given him, for you to give him praise.

This training should be an on-going process that happens all the time, you need to be ready at all times to stop, inform, replace and praise. With enough repetition, your puppy will be well aware of what he should and should not be chewing.

Keep his toys interesting:

This is covered heavily in the teething section, but it's so important I feel it's worth mentioning it again. Your pup's toys hold the key to the future health of your fingers and furniture. But, the toys need to remain highly valued and interesting in the eyes of your pup.

If you think about it, why would your pup want to chew on a wooden chair leg, if he has a peanut-butter covered squeaky toy to chew on? I know what I would pick.

When your pup becomes bored of his toys, or you're not doing anything to make them interesting, your chair leg becomes a little more exciting.

Precautions with soft toys:

Soft teddy toys are nice, but they should be kept only as high value training toys with limited access. As your pup gets older his ability to rip toys increases, so you have to be very careful with toys you give him or material he has access to.

Letting your husky rip toys is not a good idea and it will encourage destructive behavior. So it's best to try to avoid it in the first place.

Why this method works so well

Don't be fooled by the simplicity of this training method. Following the steps above is all you need to **eventually** train your puppy to chew only what he's allowed to. Yes, it will take a little time, and there will be some challenges along the way, but this method is far more productive than shouting or punishing him when he chews something he shouldn't. It's important to remember that your puppy will build valuable mental links much quicker when he's shown something with praise and treats, compared to shouting and making him fearful.

Something else I like about this training method is that you aren't trying to stop him chewing, you're simply redirecting it. This is far easier to achieve than stopping his chewing all together, which when you think about it, would be virtually impossible anyway. Your puppy *needs* to chew for many legitimate reasons and his body just won't accept that "he needs to stop". Redirection is the key, and with enough successful runs through the training, he will develop a very good understanding of what he's allowed to chew and what he isn't; and he'll stick to it. Combine this training with the techniques outlined in the teething section about keeping his toys interesting, and you're good to go!

Huskies From Around the World

This is Bruno, looking like such a good boy!
He is 2 years old, from Serbia

Husky Puppy FAQ Section – Complete Troubleshooting Guide

The husky puppy FAQ section will be the last section of this handbook and it aims to be your complete troubleshooting guide for any puppy issue you may have.

While the tips, advice, guides and training methods given to you above will surely help you, there will be times that you find yourself in difficult situations. It's normal for your puppy to challenge you in a way you didn't anticipate, or you just can't find a solution to a certain puppy issue. I hope to clear that up for you in this section with short, concise answers.

Some questions and answers will be short summaries of information that's already given above; it's just handy to have here for your convenience.

Let's take a look at the most frequently asked questions about husky puppies.

Which vaccination does my puppy need and what age?

Your puppy will need various vaccinations at different stages. What vaccinations your veterinarian recommends can also change depending on the part of the country you live in. Some pups do not need all vaccinations, but these are the basic puppy vaccination guidelines. You can discuss all of this in its entirety with your local veterinarian.

The important time when your puppy is deemed safe to go outside is around 1-2 weeks after the second set of vaccinations. This is what's referenced many times throughout the entire handbook

Recommended Vaccines:

- Distemper

- Hepatitis
- Parainfluenza
- Parvovirus (DHPP)
- Rabies

Optional Vaccines:

- Bordetella
- Coronavirus
- Leptospirosis
- Lyme Disease

Typical Vaccination Age:

- **6-8 weeks:** Distemper, Parainfluenza, Bordetella

- **10-12 weeks:** DHPP, Coronavirus, Leptospirosis, Bordetella, Lyme Disease

  ^^^^ 2 weeks following these vaccinations is when your pup is considered safe to go outside.

- **12-24 weeks:** Rabies

- **14-16 weeks:** DHPP, Coronavirus, Lyme Disease, Leptospirosis

- **12-16 months:** Rabies, DHPP, Coronavirus, Leptospirosis, Bordetella, Lyme Disease

- **1-2 years:** DHPP, Coronavirus, Leptospirosis, Bordetella, Lyme Disease

- **1-3 years:** Rabies

Where vaccines repeat, indicate necessary boosters.

How can I bring my puppy home from the breeder in the car?

For a safe car journey home, you'll need to do a few things beforehand. Having some basic supplies is important, so gather some poop bags, old towels or blanket, spare water bowl, supply of water (avoid store-bought water) a soft toy and some cleaning equipment. The standard procedure for frequent car travel is to put your puppy inside a crate, which is then secured by a seatbelt; this is even the law in some states. **However,** it's his first car ride ever and he's leaving his mother and siblings, so it's a fragile time for him. In this case it's preferred to sit in the back and have him on your lap, in a blanket. It's likely your pup is going to need some love and support during this moment so having him on your lap is better than in a crate. If you're travelling for hours, then be sure to stop frequently, every 45 minutes is a good amount. Remember that your puppy will not hold his bladder for very long, especially with the added anxiety from what's happening. Be prepared for some crying or yapping, but try not to worry too much, this is completely normal and it's just an overwhelming situation. Please refrain from feeding your puppy during a car journey, this can really upset his stomach especially with the motion from driving; be sure to wait until you're home.

When can my puppy be left alone?

In the beginning you should try to be with your puppy as much as you can, if you can be with him all day, you should be, although that is quite impractical. For times that you need to leave the room or go to a different part of the house, just ensure your pup is inside his designated room or even better, inside his crate. The quicker you can crate train your pup, the sooner you'll be able to leave him and even leave the house. After all, you can't stop running errands, and taking your pup with you may not be an option. There's no good time-specific answer for this, and your pup will be different from any other pup. Just try your best not to leave the house until he's happy in his crate and has become accustomed to his designated room. This may take 2-4 weeks after you bring him to your home.

How much should I play with my new puppy?

Playing is really important for your puppy for many reasons. You should aim to have 4 - 6 individual play sessions with your pup every day. Play time will help build the bond between him and you, improve mental stimulation and training, provide valuable exercise and keep him very happy. Remember, it's much more beneficial for your puppy if you're a part of the game too, rather than giving him a toy to play with alone. Many of the positive health benefits outlined above are nowhere near as prominent without your involvement.

Are the nutritional needs for my husky puppy different from other puppies?

Yes, nutritional needs change from breed to breed and their projected adult size. Small breed puppies will have different nutritional needs from medium and large breed puppies. Husky puppies are medium breeds and will require different portion sizes compared to a German shepherd puppy or a corgi puppy (for example). I have included the ideal nutritional breakdown for a husky puppy in the diet section above.

My puppy sits down and never wants to move when I take him outside while using the harness and leash.

Firstly, did you run through the correct leash training procedure outlined in the leash training section above? If you didn't, I suggest going over that, as your puppy may need to reestablish a better relationship with the harness and leash before going on another walk.

If you've done that already here are a few more things you can try:

- Make sure there are no other intimidating dogs around.

- Go to a park that's bright, quiet and with few distractions.

- Use some treats in your hand and try to encourage your pup to start chasing you like a game of catch up. Keep your tone friendly and try to get him moving. Reward him for moving.

- Make sure your pup has received adequate socialization before going on public walks.

- Take your pup for short car journeys with the windows open. This helps him get used to the outside smell, sounds and general environment.

- Be sure to let your puppy walk around the house with his harness and leash on a few times. This will help him get used to walking while attached to the leash.

Asking these questions first helps you to troubleshoot why your pup may be refusing to move.

What should I do when my puppy starts pulling on the leash?

When your puppy starts getting ahead of you and eventually starts pulling, it's a problem and you need to address it. When this happens, you need to stop and stand still. Don't yank him back, just stop moving forward, call his name and hopefully if he has learned "come here" as a basic command, now's a good time to use it! wait until he comes back to you, when he does, get him to sit and focus on you, while making eye contact. Once he does this, be sure to reward him with your tone of voice and a small treat. Continue with your walk. The second he pulls on the leash again, you run through the entire process again.

If your pup is being super stubborn and doesn't come back to you when you call his name, start going backwards, the way you came. Dogs in general and especially huskies, hate to go back the way they came. This will likely be an ongoing training process, and you should expect this to take a while before you go on the "perfect" walk. By stopping every time he starts pulling, it's breaking his "flow" and that's the last thing he wants. So with a little time, he'll learn not to pull on the leash if he wants to keep going.

When should my puppy switch to an adult dog food?

Husky puppies should switch at around the age of 1. But before making any switches it's best to get advice from your local veterinarian and make sure you switch foods slowly. Introduce the new food little by little over the course of a week, slowly adding more of the new food and less of the old food. Taking it slowly should avoid stomach and digestive issues.

What age can I bathe my puppy?

The guideline that veterinarians give is waiting until 1 or 2 weeks after your puppy has finished his vaccinations. This will usually be around 16-18 weeks of age. At such a young age, your puppy can't regulate his own body temperature and getting wet makes him vulnerable to sickness and hypothermia. Puppies do not require much bathing and it's recommended to limit bath times to once every three to four months. If in the meantime your puppy rolls in some nasty muck, you can spot clean him.

Can I use baby shampoo on my puppy?

Yes. Baby shampoo is fine for use on puppies. Although, it is better to opt for a mild puppy-friendly shampoo that contains only natural ingredients. If this is not an option for you, then the only other safe alternative is baby shampoo. All other shampoos, even regular pet shampoo will contain chemicals too harsh for your puppy's skin.

My puppy sleeps A LOT, is this normal?

Puppies are sleeping machines. Remember that they're constantly growing and sleep is when most of their development takes place. It consumes a lot of energy so yes, it's very normal for your puppy to sleep a lot. In fact, it's normal for puppies to sleep around 15-20 hours per day.

Should I cover my puppy's crate with a blanket?

You can certainly try it. Some puppies will react positively and some won't like it at all. The benefits are that it can make the crate more den-like, thus making your pup feel safer and more secure inside. The only way to know is by giving it a try with your pup, watch how he reacts to the blanket. And try putting it on the crate during the day before you actually require him to go inside the crate. This way he can get familiar with the blanket being there before he has to enter. Watch him as he enters, does he resist, or does he go in without any issues? If he goes in without issues, this would indicate he's comfortable with the blanket cover.

Should I get pet insurance for my puppy?

This is hard to answer and a lot of it comes down to your financial situation and your views. Generally, insurance plans are offered for puppies starting from the age of 6 weeks old, so you *could* insure your puppy as soon as you get him. However, there are some things to consider. If you try insuring your puppy at a super young age, there may be fewer plans available to you, especially premium options. On the flip side, puppies are vulnerable to illness, and who knows, your pup may suffer from some early-on health issues that pet insurance would certainly help you with. There are a lot of personal factors when it comes to whether or not pet insurance is worth it. There are many pet professionals and veterinarians out there that recommend it, but there are just as many who say it's not really necessary for "generally healthy breeds" Huskies are generally healthy, but they have their fair share of health problems that happen to be very expensive to fix. If you want peace of mind, and are able to afford it, I say go for it.

My puppy won't drink water, what should I do?

Be ready to take your pup to your veterinarian if he doesn't drink at all for 1-2 days, he'll need fluids right away. But, before that, here are a few things you can do: Start adding some water to your puppy's dry food; this will help get fluids in through his mealtimes. Exercise your pup a little more, remember his joints, bones and ligaments are fragile, but this extra exercise may encourage your pup to take an extra drink. Change the location of his water bowl. You may not realize it but there could be something off-putting in that specific area causing your pup to avoid going to his bowl. Changing it to a different corner may be a simple fix so it's worth a try. Replace his water throughout the day. In general, dogs prefer water that's slightly cold, and fresh. Warm water is not enticing. Put a treat or ice cube in his water. This will act like a game and your pup will drink water while getting the ice cube or treat.

My puppy is struggling to sleep, what can I do?

Try giving your pup some intense playtime about 1 hour before his bedtime, try to expel as much of his remaining energy as you can. This is just one part of a good bedtime routine and it can be the finisher for a lot of pups. Ensure your puppy isn't eating too close to bedtime either, food will of course give your pup energy, so make his last mealtime 3 or even 4 hours before you intend on taking him to sleep. Be sure to read the sleeping section above, your puppy should have a fairly good sleep if you follow the tips and tricks.

Why does my puppy sneeze?

Your pup may be sneezing for a number of reasons, some are not serious and some are. Reasons could be dust in the air, a reaction to something you've just sprayed like perfume, it may be due to pollen, it can even be a sign they're playing known as "play sneezing". However, there are some more serious issues like tooth infections, tumors, or nasal or respiratory infections. If your puppy is sneezing continuously then you should visit your vet, but if it's infrequent, it may not be anything to worry about. Of course, if you're unsure, visit your vet.

Why is my puppy panting too much?

Panting is a way for your puppy to cool himself down; it's the same for adult dogs too. It's quite normal for huskies to pant a lot, but it's good to know what's normal and what isn't. Mature huskies range anywhere from 10-30 breaths per minute while puppies can be 15-40 breaths per minute, so it is normal for puppies to breath and pant more often. **Please note this is when resting.** It's actually normal for a puppy's' breathing rate to increase to an amazing 200-400 times a minute. So, if your puppy has just stopped playing, running around or exercising, you can expect him to be panting A LOT. But eventually it should slow back down. If your puppy is panting far more than 15-40 breaths in one minute, when he *hasn't* been recently exerting himself, you should visit your veterinarian to be safe. Times your pups breathing may increase include: when he's in direct sunshine, in his crate, going for a car ride, sleeping, after exercise, or when he sees you for the first time during the day.

When will my husky puppy howl?

A moment that any proud husky owner is waiting for! Well, if you pick up your husky at 8 weeks old, he should be able to howl already. Howling can usually start around 6-7 weeks, and you can see your puppy at least trying to howl much before then, even though he won't be able to produce much sound. If he isn't howling at 8 weeks, give him a little more time. It's also worth keeping in mind that *some* huskies are quieter than others.

Can my husky pup drink milk?

It's recommended to stay away from milk and dairy products. Most dogs and puppies are lactose intolerant to some level and it will vary from puppy to puppy. It ultimately depends on how much of the lactase enzyme your puppy continues to produce after he's weaned off his mother's milk, but there is no real way to find out. Avoid milk and dairy items and you won't have any issues.

How long can my puppy hold a wee?

Veterinarians and various professionals have come out and said that puppies can hold their bladder for 1 hour, per month of age they have… So if your puppy is 3 months old, he could hold his bladder for up to 3 hours, BUT it doesn't always work like that, your pup will not have very good control of his bladder for quite some time, so despite this rule, you **should not** assume that it's ok to leave him. Your pup should be taken outside to eliminate frequently every 1-2 hours and especially after key moments such as eating, drinking, sleeping, playing, or anything that excites him.

What should I do if my puppy is always scared of his crate?

If your pup continues to be scared of his crate, you'll have to take some steps back and think of some alternatives until you help your pup overcome his fears. I would recommend that you stop using the crate all together, especially if he's **petrified** of it. Putting him in there when he's already very scared can sometimes just increase his fear and anxiety. It's better to find an alternative. I suggest trying a play/puppy pen. Pens are far bigger and do not have a caged roof. This will almost certainly be less intimidating for your pup. Have him sleep in the pen and put him here when you need to leave him unattended for short periods. In the meantime, keep his crate in his environment and try moving it to a different spot of the room; keep the door open at all times and occasionally throw his treats in there. This will encourage him to enter to get the treat, although this may take some time. You can also try putting his food bowl down a fraction closer to the crate, every mealtime. Try doing this until your pup is eating right next to his crate. The most important thing to remember is to stop forcing your pup in there; this will only increase his fear of going inside for the next time.

What should I put in my puppy's crate at night?

Keeping it simple is always best. Try to have nothing more than a simple bed, and a single comfort item such as a snuggle puppy toy or an old t shirt of yours. Under three months of age your pup typically won't have the strength to do any actual shredding, but still be vigilant. It's best if the bed is somewhat water resistant to make cleaning up easier. And a slightly tougher material will make it less enticing to chew. Avoid loading the crate with soft teddies, soft blankets or toys, it's not necessary and could make it harder for your puppy to fall asleep. Food and water should also be kept outside of the crate; your pup is absolutely fine to wait until the morning. If he has access to water, it will mean multiple trips outside during the night, or A LOT of potty mistakes inside his crate. So it's best to keep it out.

When will my puppy's ears stand up?

Not all ears perk up early, and it's actually more common than you think. While husky puppies usually have erect ears by 6 weeks old, it can take a lot longer than this in some cases. It's common to witness your puppy's ears dancing around throughout the teething process. Many owners report one ear up, the other down, and then it suddenly switches, this is all normal. Jaw and neck muscles are linked to perky ears, so throughout his heavy chewing and biting stage, ears can be affected significantly. On top of this, it may be dependent on genes, breeding or the growth of his ear cartilage. You can support healthy ear growth by encouraging chewing, ensuring he has adequate nutrition and vitamins, and perhaps the biggest factor, avoid fondling his ears! If you touch his ears too much you could damage his cartilage. If your puppy's ears are still down when he's 5-6 months, visit a veterinarian for further help.

P.S please avoid taping his ears upright. You don't know if you're taping them correctly, and you may force his ears to grow in the wrong direction.

Why isn't my puppy eating his food?

There can be many different reasons as to why your puppy may not be eating his food. Below are many of the common causes:

- Your puppy is not yet used to his new home and environment
- You've switched to a food he does not like. Try the food your breeder used
- You're trying to feed him at times of the day he doesn't usually eat
- He doesn't like where his food bowl is located
- Teething pains may weaken his appetite
- You're not including wet food in with his dry kibble
- He's not receiving enough exercise throughout the day
- You're leaving his food down at all times. Only keep the bowl down for a limited time.
- He doesn't find the food exciting. Try hiding a few small teaspoons of peanut butter inside
- If all else fails, he may have some health problems. Visit your veterinarian before your puppy goes 2 full days without eating.

Why does my puppy have diarrhea and what should I do?

Diarrhea in puppies is very common and although it *can* mean something serious, usually it's something within our control. Let's take a look at the common reasons and what you can try doing.

Common causes for diarrhea in puppies

- Change of diet or food
- Viral infection
- Bacterial infection
- Stress
- Ingestion of foreign object or something toxic
- Parasites

Your pup's diet and food can have a big impact on his stools. The new food may not work well with your puppy. But even transitioning too quickly could cause diarrhea, even if the new food does work well. That's why it's very important to change diets slowly over the course of 1-2 weeks. If you did introduce it slowly, and your pup still has diarrhea, then I recommend changing his food again *(slowly)*.

If your pup has recently eaten something he shouldn't have, or you found him rummaging through some trash, you can expect diarrhea to follow. Eating anything foul, moldy or toxic can really upset his digestive system and stomach.

If you haven't changed his diet recently and you don't suspect that he has eaten something foul, I strongly suggest visiting your local veterinarian as soon as possible. He may have a viral or bacterial infection, or even parasites. A vet will be able to assist you in this situation and provide the necessary treatments.

Can my puppy eat cheese?

It's recommended that your puppy doesn't eat anything diary as there's a strong chance of him being lactose intolerant. However, this is a topic open for a lot of discussion, some people ignore this and feed their pups all kinds of diary and claim there are no downsides. If you want to give it a try, it's up to you, but I would monitor his stools and reaction very carefully. Cheese is considered an excellent training treat and puppies across the board seem to love it. But don't let this sway your actions too much; if your pup reacts negatively in anyway, despite how much he loves it, you shouldn't give him any more cheese. *I couldn't imagine a life without cheese.*

Huskies From Around the World

This is Luna, looking gorgeous in San Francisco, USA.
She's 3 years old here.

Huskies From Around the World

This is Mago. She's having the time of her life in the snow!
She's 2 years old and from the USA!

Huskies From Around the World

This is Pako and Mila!
They live an awesome life in Belgrade, Serbia
Pako is 5 years old and Mila is 7

Huskies From Around the World

Another beautiful photo from Pako and Mila!

Huskies From Around the World

This is Blue and Harper. Siblings that stick together, stay together!
They live life in the USA.
Blue is 2 years old and Harper is 5 months.

Huskies From Around the World

This is Rocky, looking great in his jacket!
He's 4 months old and from the USA!

Huskies From Around the World

This is Hazel and Mishka.
Two beautiful huskies, loving life in the USA !
Both Hazel and Mishka will be 2 years old in August 2020

MEET
Hazel & Mishka
BOTH ARE 1 YEAR 8 MONTHS
FROM THE USA !

Huskies From Around the World

This is Bear. He loves being cheeky and mischievous, but not without a lot of love at the same time! Bear is from North Devon, England and he's 4 years old.

Summary

If you're reading this section now, I owe you a BIG thank you! I hope you thoroughly enjoyed this handbook and found the information as valuable and helpful as it's intended to be. After working with many people and helping them with their queries and questions, it was time to write a book, and I am so happy that I did.

I know that your journey with your own fluff ball will be an amazing one and remember to cherish every moment of it. For all of the ups and downs you're about to embark on, I wish you all the best.

It was my pleasure to write this book for you and your beautiful husky puppy.

If you found this book helpful it would mean the absolute world to me, if you would kindly leave a review. Every single review is greatly appreciated.

Thank you,
Harry

For now, you can find me posting regular articles at
www.myhappyhusky.com

Printed in Great Britain
by Amazon